CASES IN
SMALL BUSINESS
MANAGEMENT AND
ENTREPRENEURSHIP

CASES IN SMALL BUSINESS MANAGEMENT AND ENTREPRENEURSHIP

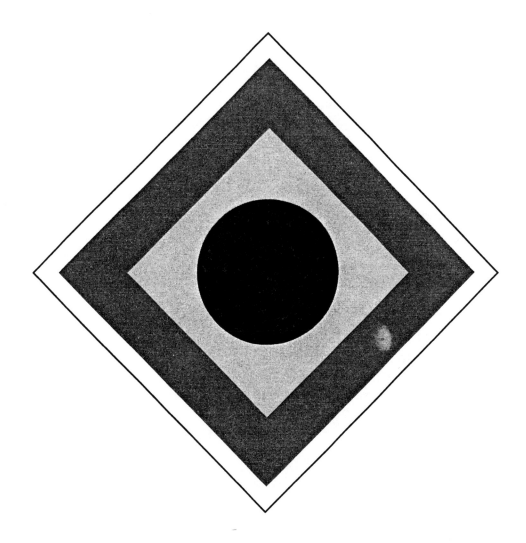

NORMAN M. SCARBOROUGH
PRESBYTERIAN COLLEGE

THOMAS W. ZIMMERER
DRURY COLLEGE

Prentice
Hall

Upper Saddle River, New Jersey 07458

Managing Editor: *Melissa Steffens*
Associate editor: *Jessica Sabloff*
Project editor: *Theresa Festa*
Compositor: *Pageworks*
Manufacturer: *Integrated Book Technology, Inc.*

Printed in the United States of America

10   9   8   7   6   5

ISBN 0-13-017082-8

Prentice-Hall International (UK) Limited, *London*
Prentice-Hall of Australia Pty. Limited, *Sydney*
Prentice-Hall Canada Inc., *Toronto*
Prentice-Hall Hispanoamericana, S.A., *Mexico*
Prentice-Hall of India Private Limited, *New Delhi*
Prentice-Hall of Japan, Inc., *Tokyo*
Prentice-Hall (Singapore) Pte Ltd
Editora Prentice-Hall do Brasil, Ltda., *Rio de Janeiro*

Contents

J. R. Pierce, Inc.

John Pierce, the founder of J. R. Pierce, Inc. (JRP), was concerned about the way his two sons were managing JRP since John "retired." John realized his two sons, in turn, were very frustrated with his interference with their management of JRP. He knew they believed that he was restricting their efforts to expand sales and company growth. Still another issue John had been unable to reach a decision about was the transfer of ownership to his sons or even if he should do so. Clearly he saw and experienced serious conflict. As he looked over preliminary results for 1995, John wondered what should be the strategy for JRP for the coming years and what part he should play.

Since "retiring" in 1990 which really meant he no longer took a salary, John Pierce had turned over the operations of JRP, a pastry forming equipment manufacturer, to his two sons, Bill and Mark. However, he continued to work about half of every day, at his discretion, involving himself in an intermittent way in die set design, writing occasional checks, and handling some phone calls without subsequent follow-up. This unplanned, intermittent involvement frustrated his sons who wanted full responsibility for this manufacturer of pastry forming equipment. John said "he found it difficult to let go of the company that he had nurtured since 1968." The sales trend had been downward during 1993 and 1994 which concerned him although the unaudited results for 1995 looked like a record year. The substantial

By Robert P. Crowner, Professor of Management, Eastern Michigan University. This case was prepared as the basis for class discussion and is not intended to illustrate either effective or ineffective handling of administrative situations.

increase in sales was due to several factors including some Canadian orders which were the result of contracts made at a 1994 trade show, increases in the number of orders some of which were the result of contacts made by Bill and Mark at the Bakery Equipment Manufacturers Association (BEMA) trade show and a large die order from a warehouse club chain. Contrary to what might have been expected, the large warehouse club order was completed profitably and in record time because 90% of the production work was out-sourced. However, production activities were strained due to inventory control and skilled labor problems.

The Founder

John Pierce, who was 67 years old, began his entrepreneurial career as a boy growing up in Columbus, Ohio during the Depression. He was able to do many odd jobs including walking dogs for people living in a hotel, buying and subsequently selling newspapers as an independent for a profit, etc. He graduated from a technical Catholic high school that offered a rigorous program. For the next five years he described his existence as an "economic gypsy." He worked in a steel service warehouse, at construction, selling steel fabrication, selling typewriters and other office equipment and even found time to complete a year at a junior college. During the Korean War he enlisted in the Air Force Reserves for three years and was called to active duty serving in the Strategic Air Command in Fort Worth, Texas.

Following his discharge, he sold valves, "O" rings and special fittings for Industrial Flow Products. It was here that he gained fluid power knowledge by attending seminars at manufacturers' plants that his company represented. He also learned and did design work on electric, fluid power, and vacuum circuits. He worked as a designer and supervisor for Sciaky Brothers for 30 months. This company had expertise in welding aluminum and titanium.

By 1964 he determined that he wanted to start his own business. In retrospect, he began selling all kinds of components with insufficient financial resources. Often he was cashing five or six small checks at a time from various manufacturers he represented. He continued to work part time doing drawing board work for Sciaky until 1975, just to keep food on the table while running his own company.

In 1968, he made his first pastry forming machine, the Model SC, which was stored for eighteen months. The process of forming pastry is fully described in the Product Line and Industry sections later in the case. He finally wrote a press release with pictures which was sent to six publications. As a result of this effort he received four orders. After building three more machines by himself, he took the back seat out of his car and put one of the presses in it for delivery and for demonstration purposes and traveled along the east coast prospecting for business. His first real breakthrough came with an order for fifty machines from Ekco Products Company who sold aluminum foil containers and wanted the pastry forming machine to facilitate the container sales. Since Ekco had no technical expertise, John traveled to trade shows to demonstrate the machine. Ekco went out of the machine business eventually but "good-mouthed" John who subsequently got additional orders.

In 1972 the Model DC machine was developed and sold. As late as 1973 John was still selling other lines of products on the side. But 1987 JRP was incorporated as a S corporation and began operations in a rental property located in Marion, Ohio.

Present Management

Bill Pierce, President of JRP, was 34 years old and a graduate of Ohio State University with a bachelor's degree in mathematics and computer science. He joined JRP in 1988 when John asked him if he was interested. He had four years prior experience working for Unocal in the management information area. He was responsible for operations including bookkeeping, shop supervision, some technical design work, occasionally filling in on the machines, out-sourcing production items, sales/pricing negotiations, health insurance and business insurance administration, all computer programming and maintenance, employee performance reviewing, production scheduling, some sales work including trade shows and cold-calling on the telephone, getting Underwriters Labs and National Sanitation Foundation approvals, and testing and final approval of shipments. He was married and had two children.

Mark Pierce, Vice President, was 33 years old and a graduate of Ohio State University with bachelors' degrees in economics and history and a master's degree in history. He joined JRP in 1987 when John was thinking of selling JRP and asked him if he was interested in joining the company. He was responsible for hiring personnel, promotional work such as advertising, brochures, sales letters, and mailings, inventory control, purchasing, production planning and selling at trade shows. He was married and had one child.

Bill described the situation as follows:

Responsibility for everything was inherently placed with both Mark and myself. In the last fifteen months we have tried to divide responsibilities as noted above. However, definitive responsibilities are inferred or implied through "osmosis" rather than through assignment.

Mary Pierce, John's wife, served as Secretary of JRP. She was there every day and performed secretarial work, sales by phone, purchasing, and collection activities. She by choice was not involved in any policy matters or management decisions and believed her husband and sons should do those activities. Although John Pierce no longer was an officer of JRP, he was somewhat involved in those activities that interested him. He fielded some customer contacts on the phone particularly when they asked to talk to him. He continued to be interested in product design although he said "he never had enough 'open machining time' or personal time to complete the two experimental machines presently in the shop."

Management style at JRP was unstructured and informal. There were no defined job responsibilities, written procedures, mission statement, financial budget, or strategic plan. John and Mark overlapped responsibilities in some areas and were able to fill in easily when one of them was out of the office. According to both John and Mark, "there was a tendency to follow previously made decisions with little incentive to make changes." For instance, the same kind and level of advertising was done each year.

The Product Line

JRP's product line consisted of three basic compression molding machines and dies, as listed below, which produced pie bottom and top crusts to meet specific customer needs and specifications from a pre-portioned piece of dough to a finished crust without scrap dough to be recovered.

Model SC (single crust) made either a top or bottom crust with each cycle of the machine. Up to 900 bottom crusts per hour could be produced. The base price without dies was $5,000.

Model DC (double crust) made both the top and bottom crusts simultaneously with each cycle. Capacity of the machine was 350 per hour of both crusts or 600 per hour of one crust. Base price without dies was $6,800. The Model DC machine is shown in Figure 1-1.

Model SCLP (loose pan) made 2400 to 8400 crusts per hour depending upon the number of pans (4–12) per the carrier which was in turn determined by the size of the crusts being formed. Base price with a six-at-a-time die set for crusts/pans 3-3/4" through 5" diameter and 300 carrier trays was $25,000. The Model SCLP machine is shown in Figure 1-2.

Dies for tart and pie crusts were typically priced as shown in Table 1-1.

The machines were fabricated from carbon, nickel-plated steel, stainless steel, and polished aluminum and were powered by an oil hydraulic system. The sump

---

Table 1-1

Size	Bottom Crust	Top Crust	Top Sealing Tool
3" and 4" tart	$450–$545	$390–$470	$150
5" pie	$485–$570	$415–$535	$155
6" pie	$529–$610	$450–$525	$165
7" pie	$545–$635	$470–$545	$170
8" pie	$545–$650	$525–$565	$175
9" pie	$600–$740	$545–$625	$185
10" pie	$650–$740	$610–$670	$205
12" pie	$860–$950	$710–$785	$235
6/time pie	$4,350		
12/time tart	$6,900		

Additional auxiliary equipment, such as stands, tables, etc., ranged from $500 to $800.

was self contained so that no oil came in contact with the crust making part of the machines. Machines were approved by Underwriters Laboratories and the National Sanitation Foundation. Proper alignment of the machine during assembly was crucial to the smooth functioning of the machine. Dies were fabricated from polished aluminum and were custom made to provide many types of fancy rims.

John said

> JRP's dies give us a definite advantage over competition. Not only is quality more uniform, but unusual rim and shell designs are possible. Because of our tight tolerances, there is no excess dough extruded out of the die which requires recapturing and reuse. We also get a more positive release of the crust from the die.

The Industry

The pastry crust forming machinery business was a specialized segment of the much larger food product machinery business (SIC 3556). Pastry crusts could be made by two separate types of machinery, in-line sheeter and compression molding. JRP manufactured machines using compression molding. The decision as to which of the two types of equipment to use was largely a function of volume and price. In-line sheeters were designed for high volume production and cost between $250,000 and $400,000. Users of this equipment included large scale bakers selling on a regional or national basis such as Sara Lee. In-line sheeters utilized conveyors and automation to minimize labor cost per crust.

In contrast, compression molding crust machinery was used by small "scratch bakers" that is bakers who were making their own crusts from scratch rather than buying them frozen or pre-baked. Compression molding machines were used for smaller volume applications. Customers might be of numerous types such as warehouse clubs (such as Costco and Sam's Clubs), very large supermarkets, cafeteria chains, colleges and universities, hospitals, cruise ships, prisons, local bakeries, institutional food packagers, caterers, hotels, and industrial food servers.

Competition

JRP had one competitor in the compression molding machinery business. Packaging Corporation of America (PCA), a division of Tenneco, was a large company primarily interested in making and selling aluminum pie pans, who made pie crust machines to facilitate its main business. PCA include Ekco who at one time was a competitor of JRP. PCA made only standard dies and would not make custom dies as JRP offered.

A number of firms were active in the contract, build to order, in-line sheeter machine business. There were two American companies, Raque Food Systems and Colborne Manufacturing Company; two Dutch companies, Rykaart and Rademacher; and three English companies, Asser, John Hunt and Company, and Crypto Peerless Company. The Colborne Manufacturing Company also marketed

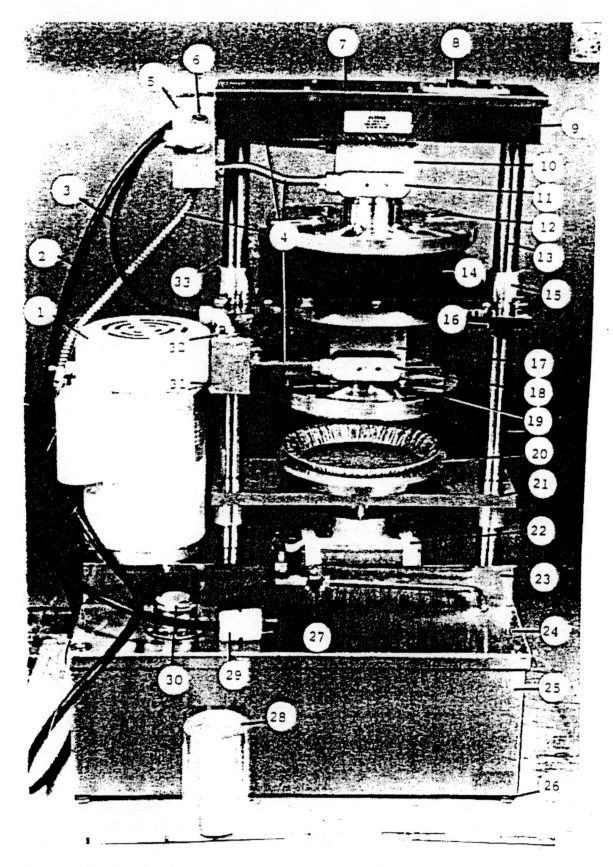

Figure 1–1
Model DC Pie Crust Machine

Legend: Figure 1.1

1. Motor
8. On-Off Switch
9. Upper Crown Assembly
10. Heater Block
12. Pie Top Die
13. Column Guide
14. Pie Top Table
15. Stop Collar Assembly
16. Upper Die Mounting Plate
17. Lower Heating Block
19. Upper Die Mounting Plate

20. Lower Pie Shell Die
21. Lower Die Mounting Plate
22. Hydraulic Actuating Asmbly Mounting Plate
23. Lower Crown Assembly
24. Base Assembly Cover
25. Base Assembly
27. Hydraulic Actuating Assembly
28. Spacer Block
30. Fill Cap
33. Column Guide

Operating the Press

1. The first operator positions himself so that he is facing the press handles. The second operator stands at the output side adjacent to the work table.

2. The first operator loads the dough portions on the poly-film on the top crust table and in the center of the pan and the pan is placed into the lower half of the bottom crust die set.

3. The first operator now depresses both handles which brings both travel plates up forming the two crusts. After a count of two the handles are released.

4. When the dies have fully opened, the following operations are performed simultaneously:

   a. The first operator removes the pan and places it on the adjacent work table.

   b. The second operator pulls the poly-film with the formed top crust clear of the die area. When the next unformed dough portion is roughly centered under the top crust die, the poly-film with the formed crust is cut free.

   c. While the second operator applies the formed top crust on a previously filled pie shell, the first operator begins the process over again by loading the next dough portions. It is recommended that the Top Crust Sealing Tool be used to bond the two crusts.

Source: Company Files

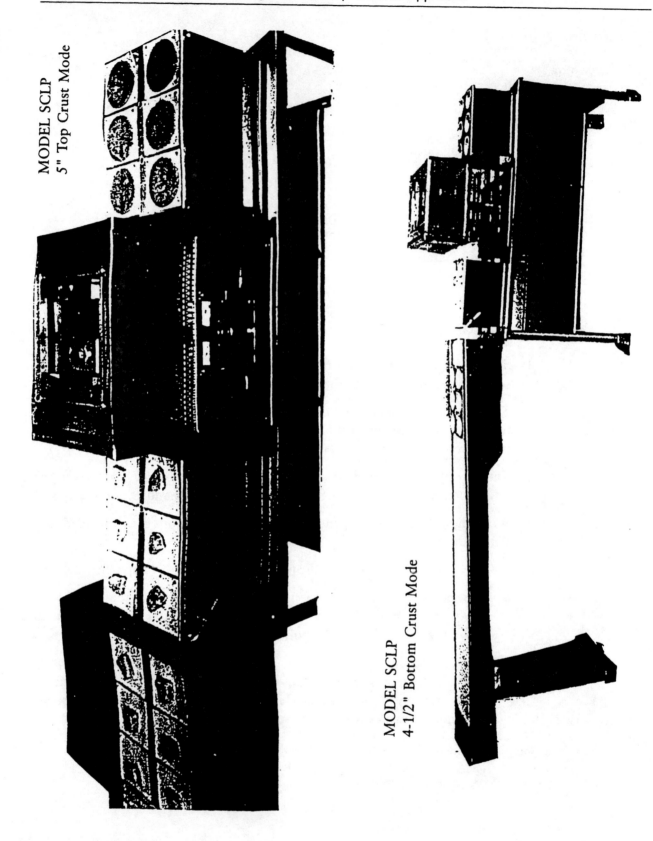

Figure 1–2
Model SCLP Pie Crust Machine

a rotary table machine that consisted of a hand-sheeter station and eight pan-carrier bases into which the sheeted dough was laid, followed by fruit ladled onto the dough. The pan rotated around the table twice during which a sheeted top crust was laid over the filled bottom and the excess pie crust was trimmed off and recovered. The machine required five operators and sold for about $38,000. It was advertised to have a production rate of 600 top pie crusts or 1,200 bottom crust only pies per hour.

The Importance of Dough

Properly mixed dough was an important factor in successful pastry crust production. Over the years John had learned much about the interaction with his equipment of various kinds of dough. He described the relationship this way.

There are several grades of flour based upon the gluten or protein content. Cake flour is 6% gluten. Pastry flour (soft winter wheat) is 8-1/2–9-1/2% gluten. All purpose flour, known as hotel and restaurant flour in the trade, is 10-1/2% gluten and is the common bread flour of Europe. There is also patent flour, 12-1/2% gluten; high protein flour, 14-1/2% gluten and Durham flour, 16% gluten. The last three flours are seldom used in anything other than bread and noodles. There have been a few occasions when a percentage of these high strength flours are added to pastry or all purpose flour to add strength to the dough for the "handle" in a sheeting operation. Shrinkage is not a problem in a sheeted dough because it is usually a couple of inches wider than the pan size it is going into. What does not shrink is trimmed off as scrap.

It is different in compression molded dough. We work from a pre-portioned amount of dough to a specific size and thickness of crust. If the dough shrinks, the crust will appear misshapen and possibly be rejected.

The uses of high strength flour in sheeted dough necessitates a high percentage of water, 33% of the flour weight, that must be well worked into the mixed dough. If not worked in, it will cause "steam blisters" in the crust and ultimately leaking pies. This well worked dough is very "strong" with a lot of "memory" and shrink-back. High ratios of shortening are used, 80% to as high as 120% against the flour weight, to make the crust "eat better" and lose some of its shrink-back. Dough of this type will not work satisfactorily in a compression molded crust. The "high strength" sought in sheeted dough is to prevent "tearing" during the time it is "flying" through the air to reach the pan in which it will be trimmed and filled.

The preferred dough for use in a JRP press consists of pastry flour, with a water content not exceeding 25% of the weight of the flour. Shortening is usually between 55% to 66% maximum, but most importantly it is severely under mixed (under 15 seconds once the water is added to the flour-shortening first stage mix) using a "paddle or flat beater" mixer implement. The resulting dough would not hold together for a sheeting operation, but does make a very flaky, relaxed pie crust. This is the preferred dough for use in a JRP machine or any compression molding machine. There is one other dough hazard to be avoided in a compression molding operation and that is puff agents separately added or included in the shortening such as baking powder or cream of tartar. These agents cause severe sticking of the crust in the compression molding die.

When customers called for help regarding JRP machines, the first thing John or Bill would review with them was the makeup of the dough being used. Suggestions as to changes in the dough would usually solve the problem.

Marketing

JRP's product line of three types of machines and required custom made dies were sold directly and through dealers and manufacturer's representatives. Machines sold in 1995 consisted of eighty-five SC units, three SCLP units and thirty-four DC units. About half of these machines were sold to multi-location accounts and the other half were sold to individual accounts. Normally about fifty DC units were sold per year. One large die order from a warehouse club chain for $82,000 was received which was unusually large for a single order.

Dealers provided a small part of the orders received. Some of the dealers were Blessing Foods, a commercial food supply firm that had a bakery equipment division. Johnson Bakery Equipment-South and J & M Specialities, which normally brought in six units per year. Smith & Wilson with Houston-Dallas offices was a manufacturer's rep that directed the purchase of five to six units per year. Reps received a chain of discounts of 3% if the customer was in their territory, 3% if the receiver taking delivery was in their territory, and 3% if the customer originating the order was in the dealer's territory. John said JRP's "mortal enemy" was the restaurant supply house since they did not have the technical expertise or service capability to handle molding machinery.

Direct sales were made to cafeteria chains for a ten percent discount. Luby's Cafeterias for instance bought about eighteen to twenty-two units per year. Price Costco, a warehouse club located primarily on the east and west coasts and in Canada bought twenty-one units in 1995.

Discounts were offered to full line servicing dealers of 20% plus 10% if the dealer did a demo when the press was installed. Call-in customers were quoted the list price but a potential discount of 7-1/2–10% was inferred if the customer would do their own start-up. Normal terms of payment were net 30 days. A prompt pay discount of 2-1/2% was given at the discretion of JRP.

When dies were purchased, the customer was required to make an initial payment of 25 to 50% at the time of placing the order. A second deposit could be required before shipment of up to 40%. This system was used to preclude credit problems with dies which are custom ordered.

Pricing was originally done in the early 1970's by determining what competitor's prices were since the costs of manufacturing were not well defined at that time. The pricing for spare parts was determined by the cost of a part multiplied by 2.35 to obtain the list price. The resulting prices had been used since then by increasing them from time to time to cover inflation.

A minimum amount of advertising, which was Mark's responsibility, was done using 1/6 to 1/4 page black and white ads which cost $450 to $1,000 depending on the publication used. Three trade journals were used at least once a year. *Bakery*

Production & Marketing had the largest circulation followed by *Bakery Buyer* and *Modern Baking* which had the lowest. Ads were typically run in the months JRP was attending a trade show. The same ad had been used for years which simply showed a picture of a Model DC machine, JRP's name, address and telephone number, and this copy - "Scrapless Production of Top Cover and Bottom In-Pan Crust Moulded Together or Singly Using Unskilled Help."

JRP has compiled a computer listing of 6,000 names from previous customers, leads obtained at trade shows and leads obtained from responses to articles appearing in trade journals. Typically two mailings are made each year to 5,000 on this internal list. Smaller mailings of 600 to 800 are made to the geographical area where a trade show is being held that JRP is attending.

Both Bill and Mark attended trade shows about three times per year. The best show was held in Las Vegas every four years. JRP displayed the Model DC machine at the trade shows and demonstrated how it functioned. Literature was made available which consisted of a collection of the three product bulletins, the instruction and safety manuals which accompanied the products, and price lists. The materials were basically black and white with one four page full color brochure and some two color pages. A video of the CS and DC machines, which was made in-house by Mark, was available which demonstrated how the machines operated. Mark said:

> The literature available is out-of-date and not very attractive. The video needs to be improved and made in a more professional way. There is no specific budget for advertising so I feel constrained to what has been spent in the past. I am optimistic that we could double sales within the next five years without any new products. But we would have to spend some money on marketing. If we could bring on some new products, we could do even better than double sales.

> We have sold products in 32 foreign countries and the potential in Europe is good. Bill and I attended a trade show in Berlin and developed several leads so we know the potential is there. There are some specific safety issues regarding having a metal screen guard around the machine in order to sell in England but this could be overcome. There are also domestic opportunities in chains such as Boston Chicken and Dunkin Donuts.

Manufacturing

JRP was located in 4,000 square feet (40 feet by 100 feet) of rental space in a industrial park located on the outskirts of Marion, Ohio. The facility was unpretentious consisting of a small office (500 square feet) with most of the building devoted to manufacturing and storage. In addition to the Model SC, DC and SCLP machines, JRP made dies to use in the machines. Machines accounted for about 60% of sales in 1995 with the balance consisting of dies and related tooling to be used with the machines. There were about twenty-six normal kinds of crust dies. The simplicity and quality of the machines made replacement unlikely but dies did require replacement from time to time.

Equipment was arranged along the two long side walls with storage shelves in the middle of the room. One side of the building contained five lathes and an assembly and test station while the other side contained three mills, four drill presses, a band saw, a grinder, additional storage area and a loading dock which was shared with the tenant next door.

Inventory control was done manually by Mark by walking around once a week for a cursory look or a periodic counting of the items in stock. A list of things which were needed for production was maintained in the shop. The shop employees contributed to inventory control in a minor way. They used a checklist located in the shop to write down their ideas of items hovering at critical inventory amounts. Verbal notification was also sometimes provided by the employees. Ideally, quantities of stock items were stored in designated areas and in "bulk shelving." When item quantities appeared to be low, the "bulk shelving" quantities were deployed, office personnel were notified, and the item was then placed on "need to order" status.

Some of the more expensive parts were recorded in the computer but Mark's goal was to get all of the parts recorded. He also was attempting to locate all related parts in the same physical area in the plant. JRP liked to have six to twenty-five finished machines in stock of which 75% were SC machines and 25% DC machines. Dies were made to order but blanks were stocked to facilitate prompt production.

Quantities purchased were based on price breaks or fifty units unless large incoming orders were expected. Most parts for the machines except for castings, stainless steel sheet metal, welding, motors and hydraulic pumps and one key valve were made by JRP. Aluminum for dies was purchased in quantities of 2000 pounds minimum. Sheet metal for the SC machines was purchased in quantities of seventy-five sets. The normal delivery cycle for castings was two to three weeks although they could be obtained in two to three days if necessary. In 1995 due to large orders, the upper and lower structural channels and welded end caps were out-sourced from a CNC metal fabricator at what was considered a favorable price.

A "production schedule" was maintained in the office which showed the date the order was received and shipped, where the machine was in the shop, the projected finish date, the machine number, the stand required, the bottom and top crust dies needed, a poly-table if required, a crimping tool if required, and the originator of the sale.

JRP employed five full time people in the shop, one of whom was a skilled machinist and had been with the company for twenty years, and three part-time people. Normal working hours were 7 to 4 PM for four days a week with a half-hour lunch break and 7 to 1 PM on Friday without a lunch break. This schedule provided flexibility for working overtime on Friday afternoon or on Saturday. Overtime was not generally required except during the October–November period when higher seasonal sales occurred. Employee pay averaged $15 per hour plus fringe benefits of about 18%.

There were no formal labor standards in use at JRP. However, both John and Bill indicated that the following figures were useful in estimating labor costs.

- A typical die took eight hours to make.

- Three SC machines could be assembled and tested in a day by one person using hand and small power tools.

- Electrical panels could be assembled in two hours.

- Twenty sets of special circuit valves, made in-house, could be completed in twelve hours.

The building was quite crowded and John had considered building an 8,000 square feet building and renting part of it to cover the payments needed to retire the mortgage that would be needed. He estimated the new facility would cost "$70,000 for land and $400,000 for the building itself." He was concerned that the new three year lease that had just been negotiated would add $750 monthly rent in the third year of the lease.

Product Development

While the product line for JRP had remained the same for many years, John had many ideas about other products. He liked to develop products and had several ideas that he would like to pursue if he had the time. In fact, a new machine, Model DCXT, was fully developed and tested in 1982 and even the product bulletin was printed. However, the machine was never introduced because John found out that the only product liability insurance he could get at the time was from Lloyds of London. The insurance would have cost $25,000 for each year of the life of the product even though only one machine was sold. Therefore, the machine was literally shelved in the storage space above the office. Recently, Bill had determined from JRP's current insurance company that the increase in liability insurance would be minor if the machine were introduced now. It had double the capacity of the Model DC.

John had completed the concept for yet another new product which he called "a walking beam" design because the carrier bar oscillated to move the pie crust from forming to a filling station. Again the machine has been on hold for some time.

Other concepts John had in his mind, which would use the basic press arrangement used by JRP machines, included a press with attachments to chop lettuce, open cans, and perforate meat for tenderizing. A pastry dough divider would be another possible product since he believed there was not a good one on the market. Pie filling machines were available but tended to damage whole fruit fillings.

Financial

Financial data for the years 1991 through 1995 are shown in Exhibits 1-1 and 1-2 which cover the Income Statements and Balance Sheets, respectively. Sales declined by about 25% over the two years from 1993 through 1994 primarily because Mary Callander, a premier pie shop, was sold to another company and sub-

Exhibit 1 – 1

J. R. Pierce, Inc.
Income Statement

	1991	1992	1993	1994	1995 Prelim
Sales	876,639	872,615	779,874	658,815	991,900
Cost of Goods Sold					
Material	206,669	177,624	178,016	133,211	284,394
Freight	12,971	13,865	10,971	8,282	15,314
Labor	142,029	153,605	155,437	138,858	140,000
Total	361,669	345,094	344,424	280,351	439,708
Gross Profit	514,970	527,521	435,450	378,464	552,192
Expenses					
Officers Salaries	69,139	84,591	79,718	82,803	85,000
Rent	26,784	30,981	24,032	25,089	24,861
Taxes	18,783	22,848	23,319	18,186	20,337
Depreciation	728	878	111		
Promotion					
Postage	3,086	4,700	5,171	3,755	2,220
Printing	4,671	3,494	5,369	4,796	3,288
Photocopy	764	285	195	170	308
Travel	1,704	5,723	110	3,203	4,655
Conventions	10,754	11,841	6,416	7,484	12,764
Magazine Ads	470	35	1,428	2,403	1,952
Total	21,449	26,078	18,689	21,811	25,187
Other Operating Expenses					
Shop Supplies	6,704	6,863	6,498	4,745	9,554
Office Supplies	828	3,057	3,092	1,871	1,296
Telephone	5,669	6,810	5,772	4,364	4,059
Utilities	3,632	3,587	4,377	3,696	3,774
Insurance					
Business	17,376	170	27,191	5,433	17,076
Health	16,530	22,869	23,553	16,068	9,807
Professional Fees	11,186	9,899	6,932	6,561	9,122
Dues & Subscriptions	3,125		4,373	3,630	
Returned Goods	4,454	450	110	1,004	2,040
Commissions	2,366	348	2,360	2,861	2,076
Miscellaneous	1,349	5,627	3,096	13,151	6,579
Total	73,219	59,680	87,354	63,384	65,383
Total Expenses	210,102	225,056	233,223	211,273	220,768
Net Income from Operations	304,868	302,465	202,227	167,191	331,424
Interest Income		5,363	3,245	2,810	3,500
Net Income	304,868	307,828	205,472	170,001	334,924
Shareholder Distributions	288,167	340,081	293,126	222,690	N.A.

Source: Company Records

Exhibit 1–2

J. R. Pierce, Inc.
Balance Sheet

	1991	1992	1993	1994
ASSETS				
Cash & Equivalents	279,531	287,668	163,582	170,256
Accounts Receivable	38,580	7,242	56,825	10,586
Inventory	25,088	26,520	25,560	29,883
Note Receivable—Shareholder	32,250	32,250	32,250	32,250
Other Assets	2,585	1,170	971	882
TOTAL ASSETS	378,034	354,850	279,188	243,857
LIABILITIES & EQUITY				
Accrued Expenses & Taxes	16,313	25,382	37,374	54,732
Total Liabilities	16,313	25,382	37,374	54,732
Capital Stock	75,000	75,000	75,000	75,000
Retained Earnings	286,721	254,468	166,814	114,125
Total Equity	361,721	329,468	241,814	189,125
TOTAL LIABILITIES AND EQUITY	378,034	354,850	279,188	243,857

Source: Company Records

sequently resold. Mary Callander had purchased 156 of the Model SC machines and $2,100 worth of dies for each machine. This order was partially canceled by the new owners. Profit margins at both the gross and net level declined during the same period. 1995 showed a decided upturn in sales of about 50% over the previous year and a return to the previous profit margins experienced in 1991 and 1992. Gross profit on dies was about 50% as compared to 75% for machines. The balance sheet showed no fixed assets because all machinery and equipment was fully depreciated.

An outside CPA prepared the year-end statements for JRP. Bill maintained financial data on his computer, one of three in the office, and could produce estimates of interim statements if desired. John still maintained a manual sales ledger of purchases by invoice number and customer, which he began in 1969. He liked to do this since it also served as a history file by machine and was useful as a quick reference for Accounts Receivable.

Two-thirds of the stock in JRP was still held by John. Bill and Mark each held one sixth of the stock. There was no plan developed for further transfer or purchase of stock. John mentioned that he thought JRP was worth $1,200,000 based on book value. Both Bill and Mark drew salaries of $31,000 per year for 1994 and

1995. They had to pay their own health insurance costs as individuals because the IRS would not allow benefits to owners of an S corporation to be paid by the corporation.

John had typically distributed funds to shareholders that were equal to or greater than JRP's net income. He intended to continue this practice although his sons questioned the need to do this.

Management Thoughts for the Future

Bill described his thoughts about the future of the company this way.

> We need a vision and mission statement. In a sense we are like a rowboat drifting without oars. How do the Pierces' do business and measure success? The present answer seems to be we don't. We need performance expectations and tangible measurements, job descriptions and defined responsibilities, and a reward system with incentives. Certainly a key element is dependable employees who can take instructions and contribute ideas. I would like to see a mini-network for our three computers. Although our equipment is adequate for our present needs, some of it needs to be tuned up and perhaps some better used equipment purchased. We could even consider a scaled down CNC machine such as the "E-Z-Path" from Bridgeport which sells for $40,000 to $50,000. In effect, it functions as a lathe without a machinist at a higher rate of production.

Bill noted that "he was suffering from burnout after a year of working 75 hours per week in order to expedite the flow of increased business through the shop." He personally did some of the die work. The large die order was accomplished by working Saturdays to avoid interfering with normal business. Bill arranged to have 90% of the die work subcontracted. Even with the outside work and overtime, JRP grossed 55 to 60% on the order. He was frustrated with the slow pace of changes being made.

Mark had similar thoughts but also some which were specific to the areas he covered.

> I would like to get all of our parts on the computer for inventory control and purchasing. Material in the shop needs to be organized in a more logical order. We need standards to use in scheduling production through the shop. Marketing tools need to be developed including sales representation through dealers or manufacturer's reps in some areas. We need to develop a budget that we all buy into including Dad. This would set the stage for increasing our sales in a dramatic way. I have some ideas I am ready to run with.

Both Bill and Mark commiserated with each other about their frustrations with their father and the uncertainties they faced regarding their future management of JRP. Both said they were nearing the point of leaving JRP. Each believed that their education and experience would enable them to get another job, probably at higher pay, without much difficulty. Yet they said "they were reluctant to take this step because of the potential they saw for JRP and all of the effort they had expended over the years."

In addition to his "retirement" from JRP, John had other forward plans to consider. Although his health currently was good, he had had a kidney removed and had undergone open heart surgery. He had three other sons, one older who was married without children and two younger who were not married. None of the three were interested in entering the business. All of them were college graduates and employed in responsible positions with established companies. He was mindful that these sons and, of course, his wife needed to be considered in his overall estate planning.

John, too, had been thinking about the future direction of the company. Since he had grown with the company, he was not inclined toward formal planning. After all, he had only had to answer to himself. He recognized that things were different now that he had "retired." He liked to do product development work and he enjoyed personal contacts as well as spending time at their second home on Lake Erie.

John had begun talking with Bill and Mark together with a lawyer and accountant in 1994 about a management succession plan that was to include a buy/sell agreement. Bill and Mark were puzzled when John abruptly broke off the discussions with no conclusions reached. Different ideas on the succession issue were raised on three other occasions but also dropped. John recently talked about creating an ESOP (Employee Stock Option Plan) plan that would involve his sons and perhaps other key employees so that the company could buy him out sooner than previously discussed for the buy/sell agreement. He believed "his continuing to play a role in the business would lead to a great deal of internal conflict in the areas of accounts receivable, production scheduling, and overall accounting and advertising." John said "he intended to totally withdraw from the company when all of this was accomplished."

CompuSound Inc.

O n a Sunday evening in late February 1995, Bob Norman reviewed his notes from his latest meeting with CompuSound Inc.'s Board of Directors. He had mixed emotions. He recognized that the discipline being imposed by the Board would ultimately result in a stronger CompuSound, the Kanata, Ontario, company he had founded in May 1992. At the meeting, the Board had mandated hiring a Vice President of Marketing for CompuSound. The Board's choice was a friend of the Chairman.

Bob was confident and somewhat relieved that the new VP of Marketing would be starting on Monday morning. Hopefully the pressure to gain shelf space and international distribution for CompuSound's critically acclaimed "CompuSound Pro" sound board would not be entirely on Bob's shoulders. Bob was generally in agreement with the addition of this new marketing executive. However, it would take a lot more sound board sales to cover the $50,000 Cdn. annual salary. This figure did not include $30,000 in travelling expenses, including a $5,000 trip to the March CeBIT '95 trade show in Germany. The new VP needed this immediate exposure to the sound board industry, as his experience was unrelated to the computer industry.

Bob reflected on the progress and changes that his young company had undergone in its short history. CompuSound had launched the "CompuSound Pro," its main product, at the March CeBIT '94 trade show. During the remainder of 1994, "CompuSound Pro" had received very favorable reviews from many in the computer trade press, which prompted a deluge of interest from potential customers,

---

By James L. Bowey and Kimberly I. McKell, Bishop's University (Lennoxville, Québec). This case is intended for use as the basis for class discussion rather than to illustrate the effective or ineffective handling of a managerial situation. All events and individuals in this case are real and essential relationships are maintained, but people and company names have been disguised.

the PC industry, competitors, and even suppliers who wanted to license CompuSound technology.

Bob was convinced that the addition of the new VP would help to settle many issues, including possible product repositioning. He recognized that any changes in the market position of CompuSound's sound board would entail rethinking the distribution and pricing strategies. Bob was also very concerned with how quickly the competition might replicate the "CompuSound Pro" sound board. Unless Bob escalated product development efforts, the "CompuSound Pro" would remain the company's only product. The amount of additional R&D required would be a function of the efficiency of the R&D team.

Additional R&D and marketing efforts might be difficult to fund, however. The company had nearly exhausted its initial shareholder capital. Fortunately, there did not seem to be a shortage of interested investors, including a local venture capital group. However, the potential investors all had differing conditions for making additional investments. There were potential government financing sources. However, Bob wondered if the time and effort required to attract financing from the government would be worth it.

Bob was convinced that CompuSound's profit potential was enormous. He stated "CompuSound has all the ingredients for success but the investors take constant convincing and the number of meetings I've been attending to restructure our finances are affecting our daily operations, especially marketing." He believed that the Board of Directors, now major shareholders, would be patient, provided he could present a new approach. Bob planned to discuss these and other issues with his new VP of Marketing on Monday morning.

PC Sound Board Industry Development

When personal computers were first introduced, sound was available only through their internal speakers. The resulting sound was crude and unpleasant to the ear. It did little to enhance software applications. This situation changed in 1988, when a company named Ad Lib introduced the first Frequency Modulation (FM) synthesis sound board, using the Yamaha OPL2 chip. For the first time, sound was played through an external speaker; this breakthrough enhanced PC sound considerably. Soon after, Creative Labs of California introduced its first "Sound Blaster" board which incorporated 8-bit FM synthesis. Creative Labs then replaced its 8-bit board with a 16-bit board. Sound quality quickly improved and the sound board industry grew rapidly.

The latest technological breakthrough in the sound board industry was the incorporation of a process called wavetable synthesis. In this process, the computer used recordings of actual instruments to reproduce sound rather than trying to replicate instrumental sound using FM synthesis. A trumpet sound was an actual trumpet with wavetable synthesis, not a poor FM synthesis imitation. Wavetable synthesis allowed personal computers to generate nearly CD quality sound.

The "CompuSound Pro" combined both wavetable synthesis and FM synthesis and also used the new generation Yamaha OPL4 chip. The "CompuSound Pro" incorporated its own proprietary chip that integrated the technologies on a single board. This combination allowed consumers to generate all-round superior sound. This capability had positioned the "CompuSound Pro" board at the forefront of PC sound technology and was a source of pride for everyone at the company.

Company background

CompuSound Inc. was founded as a sole proprietorship in May 1992, by Bob Norman. Bob spent the first 15 years of his business career as a chartered accountant. He spent the next ten years running his own niche market, computer software business with several colleagues. Over the years, Bob accumulated numerous contacts in the personal computer industry, particularly in the engineering and manufacturing of printed circuit boards. The start-up capital for CompuSound, a young basement operation, came from Bob's May 1991 sale of his position in the computer software business to a public company. A year later, in May 1992, Bob turned his attention and capital to the development of a sound board that would out-perform the less-than-adequate products that were available on the market. Bob had always had an ear for music and sound. His favorite hobby was tinkering with computers and he wanted to apply his knowledge to meet other enthusiasts' needs.

Additionally, Bob Norman had an intense love for music technology that was not being satisfied by the market leader, "Sound Blaster." Although "Sound Blaster" held a virtual monopoly in the PC sound market, its sound quality was not up to Bob's standards. Beyond "Sound Blaster," there seemed to be high quality sound boards on the market, but their prices were prohibitively expensive.

One of the reasons that Bob felt there was a major market in this area was the speed at which the demand for multimedia capabilities (simultaneous video, audio, and text functions) seemed to be converging with the demand for personal computers. All PC market trends looked to be pointing towards sound and CD-ROM drive peripherals or optional add-on accessories. The extraordinary demand for sound technology was being driven by the explosion of computer video games. The sophisticated software of these games and the marketing skills of companies such as Nintendo and Sega Genesis initiated the rapid development of PC sound capability.

Bob was convinced that he could deliver a better product at a lower price, particularly because one of the original industry leaders, Ad Lib, had gone bankrupt in 1991. According to Bob, "Ad Lib developed a terrific sound board, but its inability to meet delivery schedules and inadequate financing was largely responsible for the company's failure." Bob immediately hired AudioTech, the electronics and software engineering firm that had designed Ad Lib's technology. The AudioTech engineers had set an industry standard in personal computer sound technology and had over seven years of experience with sound board technology. CompuSound developed its relationship with AudioTech, which was located only two hours away, into an exclusive alliance. AudioTech headed the research, design, and development effort for CompuSound under the close direction of Bob Norman.

CompuSound's products were manufactured by a local circuit board assembly company, FLEX Assemblers. CompuSound had managed to merge the brilliant sound technology of AudioTech and the manufacturing skills of FLEX Assemblers to create a state of the art sound board. CompuSound protected itself by securing exclusive ownership of AudioTech's sound technology. Although CompuSound was responsible for any raw materials and other inventories that FLEX Assemblers had acquired on its behalf, it was free to have its products manufactured elsewhere.

As of February 1995, CompuSound Inc. employed seven people, of whom three were dedicated to the technical side of the business. The staff included a product specialist, a technical support specialist, a product tester, a managerial accountant, a secretary, a receptionist, and a part-time shipping clerk. Except for the accountant, most of the staff were employed in their first serious jobs at CompuSound. In terms of industry knowledge, the skills of the 22 year-old product specialist were exceptional. Bob had become increasingly dependent on the product specialist for insight into the quickly changing sound board industry. The product specialist also ran his own "Internet provider" business in his spare time, although the Internet activities sometimes conflicted with his responsibilities for taking sales calls and generating publicity for the "CompuSound Pro."

Generally, Bob was very proud of his young, committed group of computer enthusiasts. He had personally trained his technical assistants, although he had to admit that their love and understanding of computers, especially the game applications, had proved invaluable to product improvements. Since the company's inception, Bob had handled the sales and marketing functions.

CompuSound's sales had not been encouraging to date. The company only sold 1,500 units over the prior ten month period. However, Bob knew the "CompuSound Pro" sound board was unquestionably the best all round product on the market. According to several industry experts, there was no other sound board with all of the features of the "CompuSound Pro." This seemed to be verified by a slight increase in European orders, as well as interest in licensing CompuSound's proprietary technology. By February 1995, European orders surpassed domestic business. CompuSound had initially visited Europe with an appearance at the March CeBIT '94 trade show in Germany. This trade show resulted in orders from a German distributor in the music channel. In contrast to North American sales, European export orders had been met with little price resistance. CompuSound also met with Philips Electronics of the Netherlands representatives at the show. Philips was also very interested in licensing CompuSound's technology. As of February 1995, the majority of CompuSound sales had come from distributors Bob had met at trade shows. Bob reiterated his claim at the February 1995 shareholder's meeting, "After almost three years of dedication and over $1.0 million of development investment, CompuSound Inc. is about to capitalize on the multimedia superhighway frenzy."

PC Peripheral market

Multimedia was the growing trend for personal computers in the 1990s. A multimedia computer incorporated a CD-ROM drive, a sound board, and speakers. Consumers could obtain multimedia capabilities by: purchasing computers that came 'multimedia-ready' from the manufacturer; upgrading their older personal computers with a multimedia upgrade kit; or buying a CD-ROM drive and sound board separately. The best prices were usually, but not always, obtained by purchasing either a 'multimedia-ready' computer or an upgrade kit. Consumers also had the option of purchasing an 'optional upgrade' at the original equipment manufacturer (OEM) level. The 'optional upgrade' option was s small portion of the sound board market and was primarily offered by mail order OEM's such as Gateway 2000.

The technology of the personal computer peripheral market had simply exploded over recent years. Computer environments that integrated audio, graphics, video, and other media had become the norm. In the mid-1990s, consumers expected multimedia capabilities from their personal computers, although they had difficulty keeping up with the latest technological trends. Consumers were often unsure of the quality, value, and technical differences of the peripherals needed for multimedia capability.

The PC market was broken down into 'informed' buyers and 'uninformed' buyers. The 'informed' buyers were in the minority. Informed multimedia buyers were characterized by their: higher income level, higher expenditure on hardware and software technology, a tendency to look beyond traditional retail channels for their multimedia purchases, and/or a tendency to purchase at computer specialty retail stores or through direct mail (Link Resources 1993, Home Media Consumer Survey).

As a rule of thumb, consumers who purchased multimedia-ready computers, simply wanted multimedia capabilities. They were not concerned with having the best CD-ROM drive or the best sound board, but were instead in search of the best cost deal. Consumers who upgraded through a multimedia kit were also looking for a good price. Usually, when a kit was sold, either the sound board or the CD-ROM drive was the featured product. As a result, there were virtually no high quality multimedia upgrade kits that offered a top-notch CD-ROM drive and a superior sound board. Upgrading through buying all the components separately was the most expensive option. Computer owners were doing so because they wanted superior product quality. Either they had specific needs (for example, musicians) or they simply wanted to have the best quality product.

The average prices of sophisticated PC systems equipped with multimedia capabilities were tumbling (See Exhibit 2-1). Multimedia add-on equipment and kit prices were subject to similar price pressures. With these price decreases, world-wide multimedia unit sales were expected to experience significant growth. In 1993, the USA dominated the demand for multimedia kit shipments and PCs shipped with sound capabilities, with 70% of worldwide market share. Europe followed, with 15% market share, and this percentage was expected to increase to 20% by 1996. Japanese end-users accounted for 10% of the remaining market share (Dataquest: February 1994 World Estimates).

Sound Board Market

Until February 1995, the sound board industry had grown quite rapidly, making it an attractive industry that had lured several new competitors. These competitors had introduced a wave of new sound board products in the Fall of 1994. Some industry experts believed that the prospects for continued market growth were good, however the market forecasts were mixed. One projection anticipated a 1995 increase and decline thereafter (See Exhibit 2-2). Bob was slightly concerned about the Dataquest figures. He stated, "The 'CompuSound Pro' does not compete in the low end sound board market. Low end sound boards will possibly be replaced by sound chips, and I think that this might cause an overall decline in sound board sales in a couple of years."

Some experts agreed that the major argument for this potential decline was that the original equipment manufacturers (OEMs) were increasingly manufacturing personal computers with sound capabilities. Additionally, OEM's might soon be replacing sound board technology with a chip on the motherboard, eliminating the need for a separate sound board altogether. Sound board manufacturers would then be faced with a new marketing challenge, how to get consumers to upgrade the sound capabilities that were already present in their personal computers. Once the motherboard chip incorporated sound, the majority of the residual sound board market would be for high-end sound boards that catered to consumers who desired unusual capabilities adapted to their specific needs.

By February 1995, Bob believed that the markets remaining for the "CompuSound Pro" seemed to be: a) OEM based on delivery of a low-priced, high performing sound board (or licensing of technology), b) as an enhanced hardware add-on, or c) as a product for very high end music enthusiasts. Bob was convinced that his company would have at least two years before a sound chip on the motherboard could compete with the "CompuSound Pro" in terms of sound quality.

The increased competition of the Fall of 1994 had also forced a decline in the price of sound boards. Bob had noticed many new competitors at the November COMDEX '94 trade show in the United States (See Exhibit 2-3). By February 1995, there was a significant gap between the manufacturer's suggested retail price and the 'street' price at which a sound board was actually sold. Margins had been squeezed, particularly in the low-end market.

The sound board market was separated into three different price segments: low, medium, and high-end. High-end boards, like the "CompuSound Pro", all incorporated wavetable synthesis technology. One problem with incorporating wavetable synthesis was that the public did not fully understand and appreciate this technology. Most consumers, even those very knowledgeable about computers, often did not understand the difference between one sound board and another. Consumers, due to their lack of product knowledge, bought either multimedia-ready computers or whatever salespeople recommended to them. As a result, reviews in trade magazines carried much weight in the consumer purchase decision. Consumers had struggled to keep up with technology changes and had been forced to trust the reports of computer experts to keep them informed. Many retail store employees were surprisingly uneducated about sound boards, referring to trade magazine review to help them make 'expert' recommendations. Certainly a major hurdle for any sound board company was consumer, retailer and distributor education.

Marketing

Due to the lack of consumer education about sound board quality, product marketing played a larger role than product performance in the industry. Aggressive marketing and sales promotion expenditures were key to gaining distribution access and successful product sell through. Quite often, consumers simply bought whatever was on display in retail stores. Bob was sometimes quite frustrated when he went to check out the CompuSound's retail competition. "How," he asked, "can people buy this garbage? The competition's quality and features are not even close to the 'CompuSound Pro'".

Retailers typically carried one to three different sound boards in their stores. The sound boards were often bundled into multimedia kits. California's Creative Labs dominated the furious war for shelf-space, with its line of sound boards called "Sound Blaster". Sound Blaster had an enormous advantage because of its early positioning in the industry, as well as its excellent sales promotion and advertising skills. Sound Blaster compatibility had become a standard within the sound board industry, leading to further brand name exposure. Consumers had become very familiar with the Sound Blaster brand and asked for it by name. Sound Blaster's extraordinary brand awareness had almost reached generic status.

Sound Blaster also offered a complete line of sound boards ranging from low to high-end. Its high-end wavetable board called "AWE32" was the direct competitor of the "CompuSound Pro". Sound Blaster employed a very effective strategy of bundling its sound boards with well targeted and attractive software packages. Many retailers could carry Sound Blaster as their only product line and satisfy all the perceived needs of the consumers. Retailers had deemed the best sound boards to be the ones that were the easiest to move off their shelves.

The three main sound board selling points had become: sound quality, compatibility, and expandability. Sound quality was classified into two distinct categories, FM synthesis and wavetable synthesis boards, with wavetable synthesis providing clearly superior sound quality. Within these categories, however, consumers had to hear the sound boards for themselves to distinguish their sound quality. The compatibility feature of sound boards was important because the more systems that a sound board was compatible with, the less constrained the consumer's choice was when choosing future software applications. Upgrade features were also valued because they allowed consumers to add-on features to their boards as they became available. This provided consumers with some assurance that their boards would not become obsolete.

Market Segments

There was little publicly available data on the sound board industry. During the last twelve months, press releases from various companies included the following:

- March 1994: Creative Labs introduced the Creative AWE32 sound board

- June 1994: The "CompuSound" Pro received the 'Candy Man' seal

- January 1995: Turtle Beach Systems introduced the Tropez sound card

Independent data revealed that more than 80 per cent of sound boards were shipped to the home market in 1994 (Dataquest: February 1994 Worldwide Estimates). The home market was comprised of people using personal computers in their homes, instead of at work. The CompuSound team estimated that the sound board industry was broken down into three main market segments; the Home and Games Market (70%), the Business and Multimedia Market (25%), and the Musician Market (5%). These markets had the following distinct sound board purchase priorities:

Table 2-1

	1 = Most Important, 5 = Least Important				
MARKET	Price Price	Sound Quality	Bundled Softward	Bundled Hardware	Compatibility
Business/Multimedia	4	3	1	2	5
Home/Games	1	5	3	4	2
Musician	3	1	2	4	5

(CompuSound Inc., Internal Report Based on Bob Norman's Observations, September 1994)

The business market required custom-tailored hardware to meet distinct needs, along with full turnkey multimedia software presentation packages. Manufacturers generally had to service the business market through traditional distributors. These distributors in turn serviced value-added retailers (VARs) and multimedia houses. The business market also bought basic computer equipment, sound capabilities, and PC peripherals from large retail chains. These chains were supplied by these same distributors and sometimes directly with the manufacturers themselves. Several industry experts felt that sound quality was becoming more important to the business market, due to the growth in voice recognition and video conferencing software applications.

Home users required sound technology that was easily installed, problem-free, and that met their perceived needs. Gamers, an integral part of the home market, wanted sound capabilities that exploited their game audio capabilities to the fullest, at a low price. Retailers were usually pressured by the home market for very competitive prices and both the large retail chains and distributors were forced to work on low margins. As a result, distributors and retailers were not very interested in educating the home consumer about the feature comparability between sound board brands, preferring that manufacturers pull their brands through the channel.

The music market was distinct because musicians tended to ignore any sound technology made for the masses. Musicians also required specific audio features to meet their composing requirements. They mainly purchased their sound boards in specialist music shops that were supplied by music distributors. Retailers in the music segment spent time with their customers comparing various features, because sound quality and specific software were critical to purchase decisions.

Distributors in both the PC and music channels were quite powerful, and had a tendency to send goods back to the manufacturers that did not sell through to the retailers. As the margins became increasingly squeezed throughout the distribution channels, manufacturers had to shoulder more of the responsibility of communicating their product features to retailers and consumers. This function was traditionally that of the distributors.

Competition

The sound board industry was dominated by three companies who accounted for 95 per cent of the entire market (See Exhibit 2-4). Creative Labs (Sound Blaster), which sourced from Singapore, completely dominated the low end of the sound board industry. Overall Sound Blaster accounted for about 60 per cent of sound board sales. The other major competitors, Aztech Labs and Media Vision, controlled 17 and 18 per cent of the market respectively. Media Vision had expanded to take on other ventures in the computer peripherals' industry. This strategy met with disastrous results and nearly forced Media Vision into bankruptcy in 1994. Additionally, there were several other competitors that competed within the high-end sound board field, notably Turtle Beach, Roland, Advanced Gravis, and Ensoniq (See Exhibit 2-3).

In the high-end sound board segment, sound quality was the primary issue rather than price. Technological advances had forced competitors at the high-end to constantly improve their products. One industry expert suggested that the product life cycle for a high-end product was about two years. Niche strategies were often successful in the high-end sound board market. Roland had successfully catered to the needs of aspiring musicians, by offering a package that enabled the PC to transform into an actual recording studio. By February 1995, no other company had tried to compete in this niche market, and Roland had been left alone to enjoy its high margins and profits. Bob Norman was convinced that the "CompuSound Pro's" sound quality was close to Roland, while delivering features needed by gamers and business multimedia consumers.

CompuSound's Product Line

CompuSound's product line was totally focused on sound boards for personal computers. This strategy was somewhat unusual compared to other competitors, many of who sold other peripheral products (See Exhibit 2-3). Initially, some of these competitors had also been totally devoted to one segment of the sound board market and had later diversified their product lines.

At first, CompuSound had planned to introduce three sound boards into the marketplace, the "CompuSound Basic", the "CompuSound Amateur" and the "CompuSound Pro". These products covered the low, medium, and high end of the market, respectively. CompuSound had started shipping the "CompuSound Pro" in volume after the March CeBIT '94 trade show, at a retail price of $395 Cdn. By February 1995, it was still the only sound board sold by the company. The company also offered several service type products such as MIDI cables (for connecting PC's to electronic keyboards and guitars), 'add-on' expansion boards, and extra software. These products were included as part of the product line in order to project the image of a company that was a full-service supplier of sound boards, as well as to ensure that the "CompuSound Pro" had maximum flexibility.

In terms of product features, Bob Norman was sure that no other board could touch the "CompuSound Pro". The "CompuSound Pro" was considered state-of-the-art because it incorporated all of the sound board standards and compatibility features. The "CompuSound Pro" had an extraordinary proprietary chip, the OPL4 chip by Yamaha, and a uniquely integrated circuit that could become the envy of the industry. The "CompuSound Pro" had unrivaled expansion capability because it could be fitted with any of four current optional "add-on" daughterboards, and also left room for future growth. These daughterboards met the evolving needs of customers, such as providing 3-D surround sound capability. The "CompuSound Pro" included many of the standard software programs expected of a high priced sound board, as well as several additional programs.

In terms of sound quality, Bob Norman was most inspired by the "CompuSound Pro's" being named the winner of the coveted 'Candy Man Seal of Approval' in June 1994. Announced in a press release by CompuSound, the 'Candy Man' had deemed that the "CompuSound Pro" was 'Candy' tested, 'Candy' certified, and 'Candy' compatible. As of the November COMDEX '94 trade show, the "CompuSound Pro" was the only sound board to have earned this honor. The 'Candy Man' was a recognized producer of video game music who would most certainly add to the brand awareness of the "CompuSound Pro".

The "CompuSound Pro" received numerous positive reviews in computer magazines in the USA: *PC Magazine* and *Computer Game Review* (October 1994), and *Computer Gaming World* (November 1994). In November 1994, "CompuSound Pro" was also reviewed well in Europe: *CD-ROM Now* (UK), *WIN Magazine* and *Computer Persönlich* (Germany). The latest January 1995 reviews were found in *Computer Shopper* and *Computer Player* (USA) and in *PC Pro* (UK). Experienced personal computer users also raved about the "CompuSound Pro" on e-mail and Internet systems. In October 1994, the industry reviewer from *Computer Game Review* expressed his enthusiasm as follows:

> Gushing about sound boards is not something I generally do, but the "CompuSound Pro" is rather exceptional. Not only do you get quality sound . . . this card is so well-documented that Forrest Gump could install it . . . This card performed flawlessly . . . This card is nearly perfect.

These types of reviews from the trade journals and magazines were very encouraging to Bob Norman. However, the January 1995 *Computer Shopper* review brought into question the "CompuSound Pro's" ability to compete with the Roland sound board in terms of sound quality. Certainly the company had made every attempt to deliver the musician a product that had all of the needed software as well as excellent sound, at a cheaper price than Roland. Unfortunately, one influential critic negatively reviewed the "CompuSound Pro" for use by professional musicians, although he thought it more than adequate for amateurs. Bob was slightly discouraged about this criticism. He insisted that the "CompuSound Pro" delivered similar sound quality to the Roland product.

By the Fall of 1994, there were indications that the "CompuSound Pro" was on the verge of setting some of its own industry standards. At this time, Bob used his contacts at Yamaha USA, which supplied chips to CompuSound, to meet with Yamaha Japan representatives at the November COMDEX '94 show. Armed with his product reviews for the "CompuSound Pro", Bob enjoyed a very successful meeting with Yamaha Japan. The Yamaha people had asked if there was any possibility of licensing the entire CompuSound technology, which incorporated Yamaha's OPL4 chip. This type of endorsement by Yamaha (with its worldwide reputation in the music industry) was encouraging to Bob. Furthermore, Philips of the Netherlands was keen to send its engineers to Kanata, to discuss a possible licensing agreement. The Philips interest had initially started at March CeBIT '94 in Germany, through a meeting at the trade show. Bob was keen to visit Philips at the March CeBIT '95 show, to continue discussion of a possible relationship.

CompuSound's Manufacturing and Sourcing

Bob Norman had recognized very early in the development of the sound board that there would be no advantage in manufacturing the sound board within the company. Bob Norman estimated the financial resources required to manufacture computer peripherals as far beyond his capital resources. Moreover, like most hardware segments of the personal computer industry, the economies of scale required would be prohibitive. Even the major players in the original equipment market were beginning to move towards outsourcing their production requirements.

Fortunately for CompuSound Inc., the local region had managed to develop a respectable technological skill base. This base included a major supplier of circuit board assembly production for several multinational firms such as Northern Telecom and IBM. FLEX Assemblers, which was located within minutes of the CompuSound offices, became instrumental in the early development of the "CompuSound Pro". It had provided some of the seed capital and technology to CompuSound, with the thoughts of becoming one of its major suppliers. Bob Norman concluded that the proximity to such a major assembler was an important advantage for his company, particularly when it came to product development. However, the prices that FLEX Assemblers had quoted were not nearly as low as Bob had expected.

There was another important factor that forced CompuSound to avoid any investment into manufacturing assets. The Far East had already become a major supplier of low-end sound boards and this region's role in the industry would undoubtedly grow. Although the quality was not yet up to North American standards, it seemed inevitable that Taiwan, Korea, and eventually China would be forces to be reckoned within the next couple of years. Since 1990, Singapore had become the most advanced in the production of low end sound boards, primarily due to Sound Blaster's production base there.

CompuSound's Distribution

CompuSound sold the "CompuSound Pro" through both PC and music distributors, primarily in parts of Europe and Canada. The European market was especially pleased with the high quality of the "CompuSound Pro" and was less suscep-tible to the marketing hype promoted by Sound Blaster. The "CompuSound Pro" was found in over 250 stores in Canada, including Future Shop and Adventure Electronics locations. Found mainly in larger cities across Canada, Future Shop was a computer superstore concept, while Adventure Electronics was a large national retail chain for electronic goods. Bob Norman wanted to increase CompuSound's share of the American market. By December 1994, the USA accounted for less than ten percent of its total sales, most of which had come through direct sales (See Exhibit 2-5). After reading the outstanding magazine reviews, American consumers were prompted to call CompuSound directly to purchase the "CompuSound Pro".

In November 1994, CompuSound exhibited the "CompuSound Pro" at the COMDEX Fall '94 trade show. The trade show had over 200,000 participants from the world-wide PC industry. The show was deemed a success by Bob Norman in that it resulted in several hundred inquiries. However, CompuSound did not have the sales force to deal with these requests on a timely basis. The distribution infra-structure was so limited that it was difficult for CompuSound to handle the inquir-ies made bymany international retailers and distributors. It was not unusual for a three-month period to pass for an initial inquiry to develop into a small test order by a retailer or distributor. Furthermore, these new customers expected generous payment terms, in-store promotional support and training, as well as the usual advertising commitments. CompuSound had planned to visit several trade shows in 1995, including March CeBIT '95 in Germany. Though the show cost CompuSound approximately $40,000 Cdn., including the cost of a booth within the Canadian Government pavilion and travel expenses, Bob hoped that the costs would pay off in terms of sound board sales.

CompuSound Inc. was experiencing a distribution challenge. Bob had just started to understand that, "Because Sound Blaster is so dominant in the retail stores, it would take an enormous chunk of CompuSound's resource to get onto retail shelves." CompuSound was targeting three distinct channels (music, home, and business), in three different geographical regions (Europe, Canada, and the USA). The distinct customer target markets were very similar in all geographic areas. The dilemma that CompuSound was facing was how to reach each of these segments. By Febru-ary 1995, CompuSound employed one sales agent for Canada and hoped to de-velop similar sales agents in each of its target countries in Europe and selected re-gions in the United States. These representatives would be responsible for technical sales support, logistics, and servicing sales.

In Canada and Europe, CompuSound had recruited traditional distributors, in both the home and music channels. These distributors purchased directly from CompuSound. The distributors were theoretically responsible for selling and pro-viding product support, including educating dealers, retailers, resellers, and system consultants on the benefits of "CompuSound Pro". Unfortunately, in practice the distributors had been unsuccessful in selling the "CompuSound Pro", and had been negligent in their duties to provide product support and education. These respon-sibilities had fallen back on CompuSound Inc. Of further concern to CompuSound were that sound board distributor markups ranged from 7 to 15 per cent and re-tailer markups ranged from 20 to 30 per cent. Bob Norman was starting to feel that these intermediaries were not earning their margins and were adding little value to the "CompuSound Pro".

CompuSound sold some of its product directly to consumers at nearly full retail prices, although this was a negligible part of its sales to date. The higher margins from these direct sales were attractive and the consumer who bought direct was usually a very informed end-user who had little difficulty in installing the "CompuSound Pro". Bob could not help wondering if direct selling methods might not be a more profitable approach to reaching informed buyers. The costs of Internet marketing and other direct selling methods seemed relatively low compared to using traditional distribution channels.

Another market opportunity that CompuSound was looking into was large contracts with original equipment manufacturers or manufacturers of other peripheral devices for computers. In addition to offering complete sound boards to OEM's, CompuSound could be in a position to offer them a portion of the proprietary components of the sound board and its technology. During November COMDEX '94, CompuSound had started targeting manufacturers, such as IBM and Hewlett Packard, primarily in an upgrade option capacity. However, the preliminary feedback from the OEM's and primary research that CompuSound had undertaken, indicated that upgrade options were a very limited market.

CompuSound's Financial Situation

CompuSound's original financing of CompuSound Inc., came from Bob Norman's previous business. It became apparent in early 1994, during the development of the first sound board prototype that additional sources of capital would be required. When the company moved beyond its incubation stage, Bob was forced to invite other investors to participate as the company took on the financial burdens of growth, and in the process gave up his controlling shareholder position. Bob expected he would have to find even more sources of capital in order to fund the continual development required to maintain a technological advantage. The provincial government had expressed an interest in becoming involved through either grants or loans. This government involvement was dependent on whether the company was able to meet certain export criteria.

There was also an opportunity to get a venture capital group that focused on local entrepreneurial start-ups involved, once the company had achieved a critical mass of sales of $1.0 million Cdn. per annum. In the meantime the company's bank was not willing to extend the company any more credit because it had already exceeded its limits and had broken a few minor loan covenants. Bob thought, "If only these bankers understood the high quality of the 'CompuSound Pro', then they would get off my back."

Although CompuSound's current shareholders seemed to be interested in providing funding for continuing its operations and development, the present sales projections had to be revised before any capital would be forthcoming. The original budget was now six months old and the projected sales had not materialized. It was now fairly clear that the 1994 forecast would become the 1995 forecast. The company seemed to be an entire year behind schedule. The Board of Directors, all shareholders, was acutely aware that the strategic positioning of the "CompuSound Pro" would significantly affect the sales volume and the gross margin contribution. Bob felt that one of the first priorities of the VP Marketing would be a new marketing plan, including a detailed sales forecast.

Through February 1995, the company had sold 1,500 units of "CompuSound Pro" at an average price to distributors of $250 Cdn. (See Exhibit 2-6 for company balance sheet and other selected financial information). In 1993, CompuSound had projected sales for 1994 of 19,000 sound board units. All of the potential sources of financing were adamant about the need for a detailed business plan. The Board of Directors was pushing management to complete the revised business plan as soon as possible. Several of the board members could be willing to provide either temporary or even longer term capital, once a solid strategy was in place.

Bob decided that he should review the company's problems and accomplishments in light of the various market opportunities. He was very eager to get the new VP of Marketing focused on the right priorities. However, as he began to review his notes it became clear that the next few months would be critical. One option would be to send CompuSound's new VP to Europe for some further market investigation, although the Canadian and American distributors also needed immediate attention and nurturing. The market seemed to be changing very quickly and Bob really could not wait to get working on the new product features for the "CompuSound Pro". Bob decided to discuss these problems with his new executive first thing Monday morning. Bob then thought, "I can't wait to try out my new software for the 'CompuSound Pro'".

Exhibit 2–1

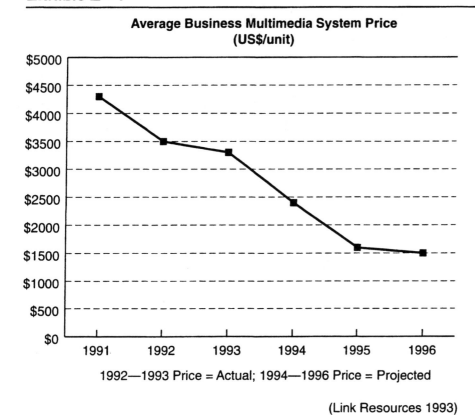

**Average Business Multimedia System Price
(US$/unit)**

1992—1993 Price = Actual; 1994—1996 Price = Projected

(Link Resources 1993)

Exhibit 2–2

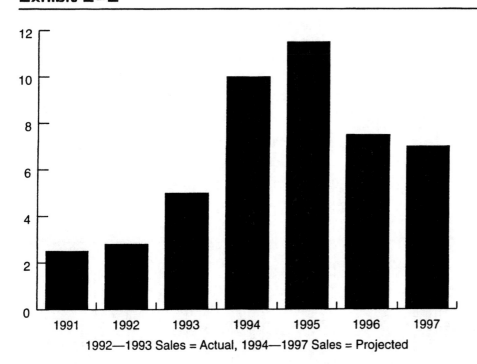

1992—1993 Sales = Actual, 1994—1997 Sales = Projected

(Dataquest: February 1994 Worldwide Estimates)

Exhibit 2-3   Selected Information on Competitors

Company	Location	Year Formed	Product Expertise	Strategy	Sound Board	Price Cdn. $	Introduction Date of Latest Sound Board	Technical Rating by Compu-Sound (1 = Poor, 10 = Excellent)	Market Position	End User Profile	How Sold
Compu-Sound Inc.	Kanata, Ontario	1992	Sound cards	Value/niche niche	Compu-Sound Pro	$395	March 1994	7	High end	Informed	Distributors, PC stores
Creative Labs	Milpitas, California (Head office in Singapore)	1981	Sound and video	Market domination	AWE32	$369	March 1994	6	High end	Informed Gamer	Distributors and PC stores
Creative Labs	Milpitas, California (Head office in Singapore)	1981	Sound and video	Market domination	Sound Blaster 16 ASP	$249	1993	4	Middle end	Non-informed gamer	Distributors and PC stores
Media Vision	San Jose, California	N/A	Multimedia, sound and video	Mass market leadership	Pro 3D	$299	1994	5-6	Middle-high end	Non-informed gamer	PC Distributors
Aztech Systems	Fremont, California (Head office in Singapore)	1986	Multimedia, sound, video, CD-ROM	Price leadership	Wave Rider	$279	1994	5	Middle-high end	Non-informed gamer	OEM, Distributors, PC stores
Advanced Gravis	Burnaby, British Columbia	1985	Joy sticks, game pads, sound boards	Price/volume	Ultrasound Max	$269	1994	5	Middle	Informed	Distributors, PC stores, mail order
Ensoniq	Malvern, Pennsylvania	1982	Multimedia, musical instruments	Niche/volume	Sound-scape	$269	1994	5	Middle-high	Infomed	Music stores
Turtle Beach Systems	York, Pennsylvania	1985	Sound cards	Total market segment	Monterey	$199	1994	4-5	Middle	Non-informed	Distributors, major chain stores
Roland	Los Angeles (Head office in Japan)	1972	Musical instruments, sound boards	Niche/leadership	Rap-10	$549	1994	7	High	Pro user musician	Music Distributors

(CompuSound, Inc., Internal Report based on press releases from various companies, December 1994)

Exhibit 2–4 Estimated 1994 Sound Board Market Share

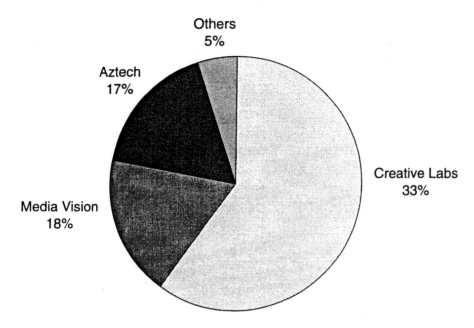

(Dataquest: February 1994 Worldwide Estimates)

Exhibit 2–5 Geographical Sales Breakdown of CompuSound Inc. as of February 1995

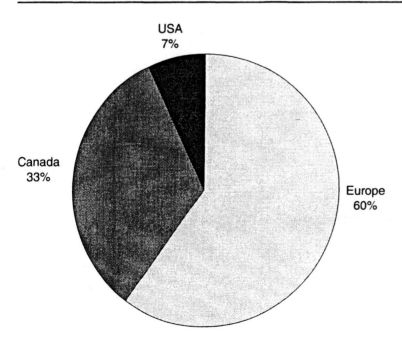

(CompuSound Inc., Internal Sales Report, December 1994)

Exhibit 2-6

CompuSound Inc.
Balance Sheet (Cdn. $)
As at December 31, 1994

Current Assets:		Current Liabilities:	
Bank account	$9,021	Bank loan	$880,000
Accounts receivable—trade	31,883	Accounts payable	835,713
Accounts receivable—others	120,623	Accrued expenses	800
Inventory	1,122,859	Deductions at source	4,191
Deferred charges	1,043	Sales taxes	196
Income taxes	84,396		
Total Current Assets	1,369,825	**Total Current Liabilities**	1,820,900
Property and equipment	73,834	**Long-term Liabilities:**	
Other assets:		Deferred credits	98,900
Development costs	961,970	Deferred tax credits	184,396
Start-up costs	81,263	Notes payable	17,798
Trademarks	5,249		
		Total Liabilities	2,121,994
		Equity	
		Common stock	899,000
		Retained earnings	(528,853)
Total Assets	2,492,141	**Total Liabilities and Shareholder's Equity**	2,492,141

Key Financial Data

Average Selling Price to Distributor/Unit	$250 Cdn.
Average Retail Selling Price/Unit	$395 Cdn.
Actual Sales to Date	$375,000 Cdn.
Gross Margin*	10%—15%
Average Monthly Expenses during 1994**	$65–75,000 Cdn.

* depending on special discounts

** including salaries, marketing, distributor maintenance, and advertising costs

Lake View Oil Change Service

The First Meeting

It had been another typical day at the office for Mike Forest at his Lake View University Small Business Development Center (SBDC) office when he received a call from the secretary.

"Mike, your 2:15 appointment is here," she said. "Thank you, I'll be there in a second."

Mike finished clearing his desk up from materials he had been reading from an earlier meeting. As he crossed the hall to the main office, Mike considered his earlier conversation with his new client. The new client, Chuck Sanders, wanted to open an oil lubrication service in town. Mr. Sanders had previously been the manager/owner of a pub located at Silver Forest Apartments just outside the city limits.

Chuck anticipated another routing meeting at the SBDC. The SBDC routinely met with approximately 300–400 clients in his branch office each year. While many of the clients operated an existing business, many others were prospective small business owners. Of those prospective business owners, most of them did not have the resources to seriously start a new business.

"Hello, I'm Mike Forest, let's go across the hall to my office."

After they got seated, Mike briefly described the Small Business Administration forms that Chuck had just completed and also described the services available through the SBDC.

"So, Chuck, tell me a little about your plans for your business."

"Mike, I would like to start an oil lube service. I have spoken to two local banks and been told that I will need to provide them with a business plan and financial projections in order to apply for a loan to buy the land and build the facility I need to start Lake View Oil Change Service."

"Chuck, that is correct. Most banks require a business plan to explain the details of the financial documents that they use to make their decision about a commercial loan. Let me show you a format that we use to put together a business plan. After we review this material, please ask any questions so I might clarify anything for you."

After several minutes, Mike concluded the meeting by setting a followup time to meet in two weeks. In the meantime, Chuck would use the business plan format given to him to prepare a loan application for the bank.

The Second Meeting

At the next meeting, Chuck gave Mike the business plan which is shown in the following section. After glancing over the business plan, Mike began to consider several issues:

What is the market for quick lube services?

What competitive forces shape the quick lube industry near Lakeview University?

What strengths and weaknesses do you think College Oil Service will bring to the local market?

If the plan looks good, does Chuck have the resources to start the business? What financial information needs to be added to the business plan to complete a loan application?

Can Chuck succeed? Why or Why not?

The Business Plan

The business plan which follows represents the compilation of a business plan Chuck gave to Mike including revisions made by Mike based upon his experience as a consultant.

Introduction

The proposed business is a fast lubrication service located on Main Street. Both local demographic information and market trends suggest this location would best meet the continued demand for convenient automotive preventive maintenance services. Presently, the area has only three such businesses. However, neither of the two businesses located on the main Hwy specialize in fast lubrication nor do they emphasize it in their signs or other advertising. The proposed business would be specifically designed to meet the needs of consumers requiring a quick lubrication/ oil change. In addition, the business would enter into an alliance with Southeast Oil, Inc. to use its oil products and would advertise this relationship and the services the business provided.

History

The proposed business does not exist. However, three specific historical facts support the eventual success of this business. First, the principal stockholder, Mr. Chuck Sanders, has 5 years experience managing a service company. In addition, market trends support the continued growth of businesses that offer consumers convenience at an affordable price. Lastly, the owner spent two weeks working at a similar business in the state gaining experience with operations, sales, advertising and promotion, and financial analysis. This training period should be invaluable to the first few months of the business.

Personnel

The Lake View Oil Change Service will have two employees and one full time manager/owner. At the present time, there is not a plan to expand beyond two bays. However, as the business matures and succeeds, plans may be changed to increase capacity or expand into additional related automotive services.

Building/Facilities

Plans have been developed into a blueprint of the proposed facilities. The business would include a 1350 square foot building with two bays on 0.50 acres. The blueprints call for two bays located side-by-side, a small office, and a customer waiting area which will include an area for handling all transactions. The contractor is able to complete the building in six weeks. Separate subcontracts will be used to complete the remainder of the construction. The outside of the building will include a small parking lot with two entrances/exits to facilitate access and departure to the store. Very limited landscaping will be required during the development of the property. The size of the property will allow for possible expansion as needed.

Economic/Accounting

The business will focus mostly on offering a 14 point lubrication service that includes changing the oil and filter. The business will also provide State Vehicle inspections. The complete lubrication service will be offered at $21.95, based upon the recommendation by the oil supplier, Southeast Oil, Inc., for most cars with the exception of high performance or luxury cars which require special lubricants and filters. Initial cost analysis indicates that the average cost of oil, lubricants, and a filter for each lubrication service will be $8.00 This cost leaves $16.95 to cover fixed expenses and provide profits.

Proforma Cash Flow Statements, Income Statements, and an Opening Day Balance Sheet are in the appendix of the case. A break-even analysis is shown below based upon conservative estimates for price, variable expenses, and fixed expenses.

Total Fixed costs per month $4,031.00

Unit Selling price per lube service $24.95

Unit Variable cost per lube service $8.00

Calculations: $\dfrac{\text{Total Fixed Expenses}}{\text{Unit Contribution Margin}}$ = B/E point in units

Calculations: $\dfrac{\$4,031}{\$16.95 \text{ per unit}}$ = 237.82 units

While the store will be open approximately 24 working days per month, the break-even point will be conservatively estimated using only 20 working days per month. This calculation leads to a break-even point for the store of approximately 12 lubrications per day, five days a week. The break-even point would be only 10 lubrications per day if the store can effectively operate six days per week. Southeast Oil Inc. believes that the store is capable of averaging 20 lubrications per day. Thus, break-even analysis suggests a high potential for generating above average profits. (Please Note that break-even analysis included covering both principal and interest on the proposed loan as fixed cash flow items rather than accounting expenses.)

Financing

In order to start operations, two hundred five thousand dollars is required. Of this amount, $66,000 will come from the owner's equity investment. The remaining funds will need to be secured through financing. The building and land that will need to be purchased are appraised at $185,000. Using an eight percent loan-to-value ratio yields a sufficient amount to pledge as collateral to cover the loan. Income statement projections based upon the break-even analysis above show that the principal can be covered after allowing for interest payments and other necessary expenses.

Inventory

The business would require only limited inventory. Oil would be stored in bulk in an underground storage tank installed and provided by Southeast Oil Inc. Construction of the storage area will meet all health requirements. Bulk storage will also keep the unit cost down as opposed to storing oil in individual quart containers or drums. Filters, lubricants for the chassis, windshield wipers fluid, power steering fluid, fan belts, bulbs, and windshield wipers will be maintained in inventory based upon projections and experience of the store manager. However, initial stocks will be based upon the advise of Southeast Oil Inc. and a similar service in another part of the area. Filters will be purchased from Auto Lubricants Co. They can supply 95% of our needs within 2 days. Auto Lubricants Co. is located in the capital about 150 miles away.

Operations

Lake View OCS will offer fast oil and lubrication changes, basic automotive maintenance, state inspections, transmission flushes, radiator flushes, and auto detailing. However, the major service will be to change oil and filters and lubricate the vehicle chassis as part of a 14 point service check. Employees will follow a standard checklist each time they service a customer's car or truck. This checklist will be documented and closely monitored for consistency and customer satisfaction. A modified checklist will be used if the customer only wants their oil and oil filter replaced. The complete 14 point service will include: Change oil, Install a new filter, lubricate chassis, check air filter, check and fill transmission fluid, check and fill brake fluid, check and fill power steering fluid, check and fill battery, check and fill windshield wiper fluid, properly inflate tires, check windshield wiper blades, vacuum vehicle interior, and clean windshield.

The typical transaction will start with the customer being greeted in the waiting room. The service associate will ask the customer what they want after carefully explaining Lake View OCS standard 14 point service. After determining the customer's needs, we will ask them to be seated while we service their car. The time to service the car will be approximately twelve minutes. However, the typical customer will be at the store about twenty minutes.

Market Analysis

The current market for lubrication services is very good. Furthermore, this type of business should prove to be successful over the next 5–10 years as more and more service stations close. National trends continue to suggest that consumers are taxed for time. Thus, any service that provides an affordable alternative to doing a job oneself has a good potential for success. Examples of these types of businesses include child care, landscaping (gardeners), and automotive repair (mechanic). The local area is part of a larger region which includes Jackson, Montgomery, and Taylor counties. This part of the state is among a handful of areas that is growing at a faster rate than the remainder of the state. Traffic counts along the Main Street have been as high as 28,000 vehicles per day, according to the state Department of Transportation. Since the Main Highway runs from Millford through Lake View to Henderson and the junction with Hwy 222 in Lake View goes to nearby Piedmont City, Lake View is almost a "hub" of sorts for people travelling anywhere east or south of the local area. In addition, several demographic factors support the opportunities for a "quick" lube service. One, as a college town, Lake View has many residents who do not have either the time or the resources (oil wrench, drainage container) to change the oil or check other vital vehicle fluids. Second, over 31,779 people live within five square miles of Lake View. Among these people is a sizeable retirement community attracted by the moderate winter weather and the quality of life of the area. The only real negative aspect of the lubrication business is seasonal fluctuation. Business is very high during the spring and summer because people travel more during these months and are more conscious of vehicle care. However, much can be done to offset this trend. Advertising and other forms of promotion can "educate" the public about the need for year-round car care. In addition, other services such as auto detailing can be offered to provide alternative sources of revenue. Specific customers for the business are all car owners in the Lake View area. Customers will be encouraged to come to The Lakeview OCS because of consistent, fast service a friendly atmosphere, and a focus on customer satisfaction. There are five competitors in the area. They are ABC Lube on Main Street, Joe's Station at the junction of Hwy 16 and Hwy 222, and Smith's Exxon on Hwy 16, near the Rainbow Inn, Smokey Mountain Exxon at the corner of Main Street and College Street, and Jack's Shell Service Station on Taylor Road. Each of these competitors does some oil changing. However, Lake View OCS will have the benefit of a combination of competitive advantages that offset any strengths that each of these competitors possess. Several specific competitive advantages exist. The proposed location will have the advantage of easy entry and exit. Only ABC Lube on Hwy 16 has a similar advantage. However, like the other competitors, ABC Lube does not actively advertise their oil change or lubrication. Lake View OCS will diligently advertise their service and emphasize the Southeast Oil Inc's name. In addition, Southeast Oil Inc's national advertising program will remind potential customers of our source of oil. As noted before, The Lake View Oil Change Service major focus will be fast oil change and lubricating the chassis. Competitors in the area that change oil and lubricate the chassis have other competing sources of revenue. Therefore, lubrication and oil changes must be worked into their busy schedules. An oil change simply cannot compete with a larger repair job, such as brake replacement or a tune-up. Therefore, their "oil change" customers must wait their turn. In addition, the competitor's prices are typically higher and the service is definitely slower. Lake View OCS will use oil stored in bulk; therefore, their cost will be lower than that of their competitors which used packaged oils. Because of their emphasis other services and products, the competitors will have a much slower turnaround time for lubricating a vehicle. Lube Shop will consistently change oil and lubricate the chassis in about twelve minutes.

A last issue will be atmosphere. Lake View OCS will always be a clean and friendly place. Employees will have an additional responsibility to maintain the appearance of both the service area and the customer waiting area. Studies show that females are a large segment of the fast oil change market. Yet, a typical female does not care to go to a dirty service or gas station and wait while their car is serviced. Lake View Oil Change Service will provide a clean waiting room where customers may sit and watch their vehicle being serviced or relax and read the paper or a magazine.

Market Strategy

The business will have several advantages over the local competition. One, the signs will emphasize the focus of the business. All of the local competitors are service stations with other customer needs that may have priority over a lubrication service. Also, the Southeastern Oil Inc name will be prominent. National advertising with a national spokesperson should give the business some local name recognition and credibility. Thirdly, the decor and atmosphere of the business will be much cleaner and comfortable for all types of customers. Often, gas stations that will lubricate your car are very dirty and distasteful. Lastly, the business will clearly explain what a complete lubrication service costs. A simple oil and filter change will be available at a different price, upon request. However, the store will emphasize the importance of performing a complete check of your automobile's fluids.

Promotion Strategy

Several means will be available to promote the business. The mere fact that Lake View Oil Change Service will advertise their service will be an immediate advantage over the competition which do not presently emphasize their lubrication services. Before opening the business, flyers will be distributed throughout the area. In addition, during construction a large sign will clearly indicate what the business will be. Once completed, the signs around the business will clearly emphasize Southeastern Oil Inc. and the 14 point check and service. As soon as the yellow pages are available, a small ad will be placed in the local phone book which covers all of the towns in a fifteen mile area. Additional mediums will be considered after the first few months of business. All advertising will emphasize the convenient location and ease of access from Main Street. In addition, the Southeastern Oil Inc. name and specific items that are checks will be stated during any commercials. Lastly, Lake View Oil Change Service will brings its NASCAR race car to town within 2 weeks of the grand opening. This promotional event has led to as many as 120 lubrication services over a two day Friday–Saturday period. This type of promotion will be done as frequently as the Southeastern's schedule permits. Other promotional opportunities such as sponsoring local sporting events or teams may also be done.

Management

The manager of the business will be Chuck Sanders. Mr. Sanders has lived in Lake View since 1986. He was a manager/owner of a pub located at Silver Forest Apartments. This service-oriented business has provided invaluable experience in customer relations, government regulations, bookkeeping, inventory control, employee supervision, and other critical retail management needs. In addition, Mr. Sanders spent one week working with the owner of a similar service in another part of the state learning the operation.

Loan Proposal

Chuck Sanders
Main Street
Lake View, USA
(999) 555-1234

October 4, 1993

Mr. John Davis, Loan Officer
First National Bank
Main Street
Lake View, USA 55559

Dear Mr. Davis:

Please find enclosed a loan application I am submitting in order to start LAKE VIEW OIL CHANGE SERVICE in Lake View, USA. The following items are included in this application:

> SUMMARY OF LOAN APPLICATION
> LOAN REQUEST
> STATEMENT OF SOURCES USES OF FUNDS
> STATEMENT OF COLLATERAL
> BUSINESS PLAN
> PROJECTED CASH FLOW STATEMENT
> PROJECTED INCOME STATEMENT
> OPENING DAY BALANCE SHEET
> RESUME (not included for seminar)

Please let me know if there is anything else you require. I may be contacted at home at (999) 555-1234 if you have any questions. I look forward to discussing this business opportunity with you.

Sincerely,

Charles W. Sanders

SUMMARY OF LOAN APPLICATION

NAME OF BUSINESS: LAKE VIEW OIL CHANGE SERVICE

TYPE OF BUSINESS: OIL CHANGE AND LUBRICATION SERVICE

SIZE OF BUSINESS: projected 1994 Sales (3 mos) $35,000
                             projected 1995 Sales (12 mos) $140,000

FORM OF OWNERSHIP: SubChapter S Corporation

ADDRESS OF BUSINESS: Main Street
                             Lake View

LOAN REQUEST

AMOUNT $139,000

TERMS   15 YEARS

INTEREST   9 PERCENT

COLLATERAL   ITEM   AMOUNT

                  Building and Land $185,000

OTHER CONDITIONS: Life Insurance will be maintained on Mr. Client payable to
                             the lender throughout the life of the loan. Financial state-
                             ments to be provided to lender every six months.

PURPOSE OF LOAN: To purchase land and a building to start Lake View OCS in
                             Lake View.

STATEMENT OF SOURCES AND USES OF FUNDS

DESCRIPTION	USE OF FUNDS	SOURCE OF FUNDS	EQUITY	LOAN
Land and Building	$46,000	$139,000		
Working Capital	$20,000	$20,000		

STATEMENT OF COLLATERAL

The loan will be secured with the following items:

ITEM(s)	Market Value	Loan to Value Ratio	Collateral
Building and Land	$185,000	.80	$148,000

STATEMENT OF SOURCES AND USES OF FUNDS

DESCRIPTION	USE OF FUNDS	SOURCES OF FUNDS	
		EQUITY	LOAN
Land and Building	$185,000	$37,000	$148,000
Working Capital	$20,000	20,000	

Mendocino Brewing Company, Inc.—1996

Well, I made beer in the garage. And we got pretty good at it. We started a fad. Brewpubs are everywhere now. California is nice to small brewers. The microbrewery industry is a good one to be in now. It's exciting, there's romance, it's the American dream. Brewing is art and science. The art is creating a stable product; the science is to maintain quality throughout the distribution system. Big brewers can do this because they preserve shelf life with no problems.

—Michael Laybourn, President & CEO, Mendocino Brewing Company.

On September 6, 1996, the Mendocino Brewing Company (MBC) announced that it had been forced to postpone the opening of its new brewery until early 1997. The new brewery, which would immediately allow MBC to quadruple its production of beer, was scheduled to commence operations in the third quarter of 1996. The company's Marketing Director, Michael Lovett, had high hopes for the new brewery:

This case study was prepared by Armand Gilinsky, Director of the Small Business Institute at Sonoma State University, as a basis for class discussion rather than to illustrate either effective or ineffective handling of an administrative situation.

We are building a state-of-the-art brewery using the latest knowledge in order to become more "efficient." We also need to control costs in the distribution and management areas. We have developed controls for production and processes, using industry benchmarks. As we get better at doing these things, we will automatically make money without spending more.

However, costs of the previously estimated $8.2 million capacity expansion had risen to $9.2 million, and the project had been delayed by a number of setbacks. These setbacks included: a longer-than-expected environmental impact review process; the August 1995 departure of its proponent, Ukiah city manager, Charles Rough Jr.; heavy winter rains in early 1996 that postponed construction; and unexpected soil conditions that hampered installation of a wastewater treatment system. The expansion project also underwent last-minute changes in design, consolidating two construction phases into one.

Lovett wondered whether or not MBC had waited too long to begin its capacity expansion project. He explained the rationale behind ramping-up capacity faster than originally planned:

That was a market-driven decision. We just felt that the market was dictating that we move faster . . . Our biggest regrets are: 1) we lost market share by not responding to changes in the market; 2) we didn't get on-line like Sierra Nevada; and 3) we didn't raise money in 1990 for expansion. We're too small for NASDAQ. Our stock price is overvalued now. With regard to selling off the brewery to someone else, we have been approached in the past but not approached recently. Capitalization and managing growth are our biggest problems. We are learning. In the meantime, it's trial and error.

When the postponement of the new brewery's opening was announced, MBC's President and Chief Executive Officer, Michael Laybourn remarked:

We could fall behind because of improper market positioning, insufficient resources, or lack of invested capital. We are currently evaluating several options to strengthen our market position: 1) continuing product quality, 2) product line extension, 3) geographical expansion, 4) improving distribution via entry into new distribution channels, and 5) adding product awareness promotion to brand loyalty promotion. Choosing any of these strategies requires access to capital on favorable terms, could incur additional costs, and represents a tradeoff between remaining a small, manageable high-margin business and becoming a larger, more impersonal, and less profitable business.

Over the past ten years MBC had grown from a small outfit run by entrepreneurs with traditional beer recipes into a regional microbrewery. [See Exhibit 4-1 for a classification of brewing companies by size.] In 1983 California became the first state in the nation to change its laws to allow the operation of brewpubs. Laybourn, MBC's founder, seized this opportunity, opening the Hopland Brewery, restaurant and gift shop in Hopland, about 100 miles north of San Francisco. MBC thus became the first new brewpub in California and the second in the United States since Prohibition. Like other pioneers in the microbrewing industry, MBC faced several disadvantages associated with its small size and lack of business experience.

By 1996, microbreweries accounted for nearly 2% of total US beer sales. By the 21st century, microbreweries were expected to reach a 5%–6% share of this market. Industry observers considered management skills, quality control and adequate capital to be essential to survival in the microbrewing business. The necessary state-of-the-art equipment alone required substantial capital infusions. Funds were needed for plant capacity expansions and marketing. Without such funding, brewpubs and microbreweries typically failed at an annual rate of 14% and 16%, respectively, according to the Institute for Brewing Studies in Boulder, Colorado.

Latecomers with large marketing and financial resources were introducing microbrewed beers aimed toward the mass market. With deeper pockets and greater economies of scale, these large competitors could be expected to lower prices to capture greater market shares and thus squeeze out the pioneers. George Johnson, Professor of Business and Director of the Craft Brewing Business Institute at Sonoma State University, remarked in 1995:

> The big guys have already started to do it. Anheuser–Busch, Coors and Miller's are trying to market beer into this 'craft' beer market. Will the public buy them? Craft beer buyers are loyal to their brands. People move into the craft brewing market and stay there. But where do these small companies get the money to grow? That's the big question.

Some microbreweries sought conventional bank loans; some, strategic alliances as contract manufacturers for the large national brewing companies. Other microbreweries, hoping to remain independent while increasing volume and sales, resorted to equity or "creative financing," noted Jack Erickson, the publisher of the *Erickson Report*, a microbrewing industry newsletter. In some cases, with brewers hawking shares "like penny stocks over the radio," these schemes seemed as much about marketing as raising money, Erickson said. At a time when a beer's popularity could be measured in weeks, persuading a customer to invest in a brewery was seen by many entrepreneurs as a means for raising funds as well as a way to help ensure customer loyalty. Several microbreweries went public with their stock in 1994 and 1995 via Initial Public Offerings (IPOs). "However," Julie Tilsner wrote in the January 16, 1995 issue of *Business Week*, "it's not easy to invest [in microbreweries]. None of these IPOs are large enough to be on any [major] public exchanges. The companies are selling the shares directly, without benefit of an underwriter, and no brokers handle later trading."

By the end of 1995, the IPOs of several large microbreweries had nevertheless gained national attention and their stocks were actively being traded on public exchanges. Notable examples included the Boston Beer Company in Massachusetts, Redhook Ale Brewery and Hart Brewing, both of the state of Washington, and Pete's Brewing Co. in Palo Alto, California. [See Exhibit 4-2 for a list of recent IPOs.]

Company History

In February 1982, Laybourn, Norman Franks, and John Scahill began home brewing as a hobby. They then took the legal steps and provided initial capital to start a commercial brewery. In January 1983, MBC acquired the assets of New Albion Brewing Co. located in Sonoma, CA. Founded by Jack McAuliffe in 1976, New Albion had been the first new microbrewery to commence operations in the U.S. since Prohibition. The venture team also hired McAuliffe, Donald Barkley (New Albion's master brewer), and Michael Lovett. The five founders were also principal shareholders. [See Exhibit 4-3 for a profile of MBC's current venture team.]

Michael Lovett recalled the early days:

> We evolved from the first microbrewery in California, New Albion. Because of local opposition to expansion of New Albion's original site we then picked a new location for a brewpub in Hopland [about an hour's drive north of Sonoma], then hired New Albion Brewing Company staff. We decided to produce beer because we loved it ourselves. We saw a market for other styles of beer. Beer, after all, is associated with benefits like the "happy side" of life.

> The original three founders are still with the company. I expect all three founders will still be involved with the brewery in five years, as we bring it up to capacity. We are team players and will stick with the company until the end. The rewards to us for completing MBC are great. We like seeing the growth process, receiving financial rewards, and insuring that our investment is secure.

In March 1982, the company leased a 100 year-old brick building, known since the early 1900's as the "Hopvine Saloon," located along US Highway 101 in the center of Hopland, a historic region for hop growing. The building was renovated and, behind it, a hop kiln brewhouse was built. Mendocino Brewing Company, a California limited partnership, was formed in March, 1983. Because of its remote location, the founding venture team expected that the brewery's retail sales growth would be limited to local customers and drive-by tourist traffic on Highway 101. According to Lovett:

> We were customer-oriented from the beginning. We built MBC in Hopland along the tourist route, hoping that the positive image from visiting the brewpub would translate into buying products on the retail shelf. We added a full kitchen and restaurant along with a retail merchandise store. We relied solely on word-of-mouth advertising, which gave us a cult following. Our original customer profile include wine connoisseurs with culinary interests who liked beer and were either white- or blue collar workers. We have been copied by other microbreweries and they still come to us for ideas.

Brewing began in July 1983. On August 14th, the partners opened The Hopland Brewery. In December, 1983, the partners began hand-bottling *Red Tail Ale* in 1.5 liter champagne magnums to satisfy off-premises demand. Lovett recalled:

They sold immediately as 42 lb. six packs. Because large glass bottle manufacturers were unwilling or unable to do so, Fritz Maytag (CEO of the Anchor Steam Brewing Company in nearby San Francisco) sold us glass bottles in the smaller quantities that we needed. Maytag has helped to maintain the industry as a "labor of love" and to save it, among other things.

By 1984 the company had expanded production by 67% and doubled the size of The Hopland Brewery.

From 1986 to 1987, additional limited partnership units were sold to private investors to finance the purchase of new brewing equipment and fermenting tanks. MBC began shipping *Red Tail Ale* in 12 oz. bottles to wholesale distributors, who in turn sold to retail accounts. Wholesale distribution was at the time the principal means of expanding sales to the mass market. Lovett explained that demand for *Red Tail Ale* soon surpassed production capacity, and MBC then implemented a policy of allocating limited supply to distributors.

In 1990, MBC acquired a 120 bottle-per-minute bottling machine. Also in that year the company hired a consultant to help management begin the transition from the entrepreneurial stage to the growth stage. Laybourn instituted a total quality management training program and structured the company into teams:

We began realizing problems from growth. Total Quality Management issues were raised as well as needs to improve Human Resources Management. We knew back then that we would have to become a corporation and, as a result of these changes, the partners wouldn't be equal shareholders anymore.

In 1993, sales increased 1.5% to $3,363,908 over $3,314,199 in 1992. Growth was attributed to brewing operations, which increased wholesale bottled beer shipments by 5.5% in 1993. *Red Tail Ale*, the company's flagship brand, now represented 84% of production. Retail sales showed a decline as draft sales decreased by 5.6%, which was almost offset by an increase in food and merchandise sales at the brewpub. Gross profit from brewing operations decreased 3.8% to $1,051,291 (from $1,091,828 in 1992), largely due to increases in labor costs (primarily wages, production hours, and training costs) of $38,000, and a 6% increase in the cost of bottles. A reduction in food costs and improvements in inventory control resulted in a gross profit increase of 1.7% to $525,752 in 1993.

By 1993, wholesale distributions accounted for 72% of MBC's total sales, of which 85% were to eight Northern California distributors. Products were sold in over 1,500 retail outlets in Northern California. The single largest retail outlet, in terms of volume sold, was The Hopland Brewpub, which was highly dependent upon tourist traffic for sales. The brewery's two largest Northern California distributors, Bay Area Distributing (25%) and Golden Gate Distributing (20%), accounted for 45% of 1993 wholesale distributions. In 1993, retail sales, as a percentage of total sales, were 12% for draft and bottled beer and 16% for food and merchandise.

On January 1, 1994, the Partnership incorporated by transferring all of its assets including its name to a newly-formed California corporation in exchange for

100% of the Common and Preferred Stock of the corporation. The Partnership distributed these shares to its partners on January 3rd.

Lovett explained that by 1994, MBC had reached the point:

> . . . where we couldn't store everything we needed to brew and package our beer. You see, cost is a factor with our suppliers for storing and delivering raw materials. Labels are a more controllable factor for us in terms of cost and availability, but glass is costly because we use very little, compared with competitors, and we tend to get the end of a production run from bigger suppliers. We expected that our leverage with suppliers would naturally increase as we grew larger.

MBC decided it needed to raise money to build another brewery to churn out more of its *Red Tail Ale*. Typically, a company hired an underwriter when it decided to offer shares to the public in an Initial Public Offering (IPO). But looking to save $200,000 in underwriters' fees, MBC chose to market the stock directly to consumers in a Direct Public Offering (DPO). Lovett described this process:

> We were running at 100% capacity and were constrained by this. We could not meet demand. Insufficient capacity also constrained the expansion of our product line. So, we hired Drew Fields [a San Francisco-based securities lawyer and author of *Taking Your Company Public*] to advise us on how to go public via a DPO, which is really an extended private placement of stock to customers and affinity groups. Fields had also advised our neighbors in Ukiah, Real Goods Trading Company, on how to do a DPO. We used multi-phased marketing to raise capital: pitching to our customers in our 13,000-reader circulation newsletter, *The Brewsletter*; stuffing tombstone notices into each of our six-packs; and advertising in the local papers. All of the funds raised would be used for the capacity expansion.

In February 1995, the company closed its DPO of 600,000 shares of common stock for $6 per share, raising gross proceeds of $3.6 million and net proceeds of $3.3 million. Funds were earmarked primarily for the acquisition of land and equipment and construction of a new brewery in nearby Ukiah. MBC's expansion plans also included long-term debt and equipment financing commitments from bank loans of approximately $4.7 million and the use of $200,000 from internally-generated funds.

The new brewery was expected to have enough capacity to produce 50,000 barrels (bbls.) of beer for shipment within four to eight weeks after start-up, and additional space was available to permit incremental capacity expansions to brew up to 200,000 bbls. annually. MBC was listed on the Pacific Stock Exchange, and during its first year as a public company, its shares traded steadily in the $7-1/2 TO $8-1/2 range but without much upward movement. Laybourn later said publicly that he had been pleased with the result of the first DPO.

On Friday, May 12, 1995, MBC held its first annual shareholder meeting at the nearby Ukiah Conference Center. At that annual meeting Laybourn told shareholders that the company hoped to close purchase of the land for the new brewery as soon as the necessary environmental impact studies were completed and that there was no known opposition to the project. He also said that the company intended to purchase a new fermentation tank to increase production at the existing Hopland facility. The new tank was expected to increase existing capacity, beginning around August, 1995. Laybourn observed that, because the Hopland brewery had been operating at full capacity for several years, it possessed little ability to increase revenues for 1995 without these measures. Meanwhile, costs associated with being a public company resulted in increased operating expenses. [See Exhibits 4-4–4-7 for company financial information and financial ratios and Exhibit 4-8 for selected comparative financial ratios for microbreweries.]

US Brewing Industry and Competition

Domestic brewing has its foundations entwined with the establishment of the original 13 colonies. Many of the country's founding fathers were either brewers or had some connection with breweries. In 1870, there were over 3,000 breweries in the US. Most were small scale—in the back room of a pub—or free-standing small local breweries serving their surrounding communities. In 1887, the average brewery produced 10,000 bbls. Mass production and marketing along with improved technologies increased competition among brewers, and larger brewers either bought competing breweries or forced them out of business. By 1900, the number of domestic brewing companies had decreased to 1,751. As Prohibition gained momentum, and as several states adopted dry laws, the number of brewers further decreased so that by 1914, there were 1,250 domestic brewing companies. Fewer than 600 of these resumed production after Prohibition, as the competitive nature of the industry increased, with the larger national brewers gaining a greater market share by buying or forcing smaller brewers out of business. By the mid-1960s, fewer than 100 domestic brewing companies remained in operation.

In the late 1960's and early 1970s, wine-drinking patterns and culinary trends changed to more diversified and up-scale products. This trend continued into the beer market and increased demand for distinctive, full-flavored beers, primarily brewed by foreign brewers and a few of the remaining small domestic brewers. The gradual renaissance for the small domestic specialty brewer began in 1965, when a Stanford University graduate, Fritz Maytag, bought and began resurrecting San Francisco's Anchor Brewing Co. (originally founded in 1896). The number of small brewers, meanwhile, continued to decline, as fewer than 40 domestic brewing companies were in operation by the late 1970s.

While the US beer market's sales volume grew at an average rate of 3% annually from 1970 to 1980, the market experienced a .9% average growth rate from 1981 to 1991. Domestic beer sales fell by .4% in 1992, increased by .5% in 1993, were flat in 1994, and declined by 1.1% in 1995. By then, beer sales in the US had reached $51.1 billion and the market was dominated by the top five domestic beer producers, ranked by their 1993 sales: Anheuser–Busch Cos. (the world's largest brewer with 46.6% of the US beer market); Miller Brewing Co. (owned by tobacco and food conglomerate Phillip Morris, with a 22.7% share), Adolph Coors Co. (10.5%), Stroh Brewery Co. (7.6%) and G. Heileman Brewing Co. (6.2%). In early

1996, Stroh Brewery purchased the Heileman Brewing Co. for an estimated $275 million.

The remaining 7.5% of the US beer market was shared by imported beers and some smaller brands such as Pabst, Keystone and Henry Weinhard's. According to The Institute for Brewing Studies, just under one percent of this specialty niche was shared by over 570 microbreweries, regional specialty breweries and brewpubs. The import/domestic specialty segment, by contrast, had grown steadily from the mid-'80s to the mid '90s, with annual rates of growth approaching the 40–50% range. By 1995, there were over 90 brewpubs, microbreweries, and regional specialty brewers in California alone (more than any other state) and approximately 745 nationwide, according to the Institute of Brewing Studies. There was a 7.6% increase in 1995 sales of imported beers and an increase of approximately 40% in domestic specialty beers. In that year, sales of domestic specialty beers made up approximately 1.5% of the US beer market, up from less than 1.0% in 1994.

This rapid growth of small specialty brewers did not go unnoticed by the large brewers. Having experienced less than 1% annual growth over the last decade, large brewers were now researching specialty beer products and entering either niche markets or markets which could be segmented to provide an added source of growth. These segments included:

1. Low-priced (*Busch, Milwaukee's Best, Old Milwaukee*)—20% U.S. market share

2. Premium (*Budweiser, Miller Lite, Bud Light, Coors Light*)—60% share

3. Super-Premium *Michelob, Lowenbrau*)—15% share

4. Import/Domestic Specialty—5% share, including:

    *   Foreign Imports (*Guinness, Pilsner Urquell, Bass Pale Ale, Harp, Heineken, Amstel Light, Beck's, St. Pauli Girl*)

    *   Regional Specialty/Contract Brewers (*Bridgeport Pale Ale, Red Tail Ale, Anchor Steam Beer, Pyramid Pale Ale, Full Sail Ale, Red Hook ESB, Pete's Wicked Ale, Sierra Nevada Pale Ale, Samuel Adams Boston Lager*)

    *   Large Brewer Specialty Products (*Killian's Irish Red, Henry Weinhard's Private Reserve, Miller Reserve Amber, Rolling Rock Extra Ale*)

Sales of domestic specialty beers were highest on the West Coast. In California approximately 300,000 bbls. were sold in 1993, of which MBC sold 12,500 bbls. In Oregon, sales of domestic specialty beers accounted for 4% (29,000 bbls.) of that state's total beer sales. Of that amount, 23,000 bbls. were sold as draft beer. Portland had more microbreweries and brewpubs than any other city in the US. Oregon and Washington had approximately 50 brewpubs and microbreweries and were considered mature markets for specialty beers.

As the domestic specialty beer segment continued to grow, the number and availability of specialty beers were also expected to proliferate as regional specialty brewers and microbrewers expanded their capacity and as new brewers entered the market. MBC competed directly with other small local breweries and brewpubs, foreign brewers, contract brewers (such as Boston Beer Co. and Pete's Brewing Co.), regional specialty brewers (such as Anchor Brewing Co., Sierra Nevada Brewing Co., and Redhook Ale Brewery), and large brewers. Several of MBC's competitors were known to be expanding their production capacity to meet increasing demand. These competitors typically had a substantially greater critical mass of financial resources, marketing strength and distributor influence than did MBC.

Similarly, the nation's largest brewers showed interest in the emerging market niche by introducing their own specialty products, purchasing the rights to specialty products, and investing in regional specialty brewers. By 1995, Miller Brewing Company was producing *Reserve Lager, Amber Ale,* and *Velvet Stout.* It also acquired Jacob Leinenkugel Brewing Company in 1987 and was distributing *Leinenkugel Red Lager, Leinie Light* and *Leinie Limited.* In February 1995, Miller bought a controlling share in Celis Brewery Inc. of Austin, Texas. Similarly, Coors began a subsidiary company brewing *Killian Red* in 1981. The brand went national in 1989 and was experiencing annual growth of about 40%. Stroh Brewer Co. made *Augsburger Octoberfest* and *Doppelbock* and produced a regional brew called *Red River Valley Select Red Lager.* Anheuser–Busch developed its own microbrews named *Red Wolf, Elk Mountain Amber Ale* and *Red Lager.* In 1995, Anheuser joined forces with Redhook via a 25% equity investment and distribution rights for *Redhook Ale.*

Barriers to Entry

Entry into the regional specialty beer market segment was, compared to entering the mass market, relatively easy. Each year, a growing number of small brewers entered the segment, while the established market leaders increased sales and, in certain cases, production capabilities and market share. MBC expected competition in its segment to intensify further, as regional specialty brewers increased production and became more sophisticated in marketing.

Still, the manufacture and sale of alcoholic beverages was a highly regulated and taxed business. If alcohol taxes were increased, MBC would have to raise prices to maintain present profit margins. MBC did not believe that this would reduce sales, but it could depend on the amount of increase, general economic conditions, and other factors. MBC believed that its position as a high-quality specialty brewer and its penetration into the market segment would enable it to continue to withstand tax increases in the near-term. Higher taxes could reduce overall demand for beer. More restrictive regulations relating to environment, plant safety or product advertising could also increase operating costs.

MBC was licensed to manufacture and sell beer by the California Department of Alcoholic Beverage Control (ABC). A "Small Beer Manufacturer's License" allowed MBC to brew up to 1,000,000 bbls. per year, to conduct wholesale sales, and to conduct on-premise sales of the brewery's beers in The Hopland Brewery. An "Off Sale Beer and Wine License" issued by ABC allowed off-premises sales of beer and wine. A federal permit from the Bureau of Alcohol, Tobacco, and Firearms (BATF) allowed MBC to manufacture fermented malt beverages.

To keep these licenses and permits in force, MBC paid annual fees and submitted timely production reports and excise tax returns. Prompt notice of any changes in the operations, ownership, or company structure also had to be made to these regulatory agencies. BATF approved all product labels, which needed to include an alcohol use warning. These agencies required that individuals owning equity securities in aggregate of 10% or more in MBC be investigated as to their suitability (these individual owners included Laybourn, Franks, and Scahill).

MBC also paid Federal excise taxes of $7.00 per bbl. for up to 60,000 bbls. of production per year and $18.00 per bbl. for production in excess of 60,000 bbls. The California tax rate as of 1994 was $6.20 per bbl. Beginning with the six month period ended June 30, 1995, MBC began classifying federal and state excise taxes as a reduction of gross sales in order to be consistent with industry standards.

The Hopland Brewery's restaurant was regulated by the Mendocino County Health Department, which required an annual permit and inspections. MBC was also subject to various federal, state, and local environmental laws which regulated the use, storage, handling, and disposal of substances. Production operations had to comply with OSHA standards.

MBC planned to operate water treatment facilities at its new brewery site to assist in degrading proteins present in waste water discharges. Permits were required from the California State Water Quality Management Agency in connection with the treatment facilities operation. The possibility existed that MBC could be held liable for contamination of the earth beneath its brewing operations.

Shortages or increased costs of fuel, water, raw materials, power, or building materials, or allocations by suppliers or governmental regulatory bodies, could materially delay the expansion of the brewery, restrict the operations of the existing brewery and/or brewpub, or otherwise adversely affect the ability of MBC to meet its objectives. Certain supplies that MBC used for production were subject to risks inherent in agriculture, and MBC had experienced minor delays in shipment of bottles, which were at the time available from only two manufacturers. All supplies needed to be transported and were subject to work stoppages and other risks. [See Exhibit 4-9 for a comparison of suppliers' inputs.]

None of MBC's products were heat pasteurized, irradiated, or chemically treated. The brewing operation was subjected to hazards such as contamination. MBC maintained product liability insurance. No such claims had been filed in its 13-year history.

MBC's business was subject to variations as a result of seasonality, which management believed was typical in the brewing industry. Beer consumption historically increased by approximately 20% during the summer months. Since MBC's wholesale distributors had always been on an allocation basis, seasonality had little effect on wholesale sales. Retail sales, which depended largely on tourist traffic, were historically higher in the third and fourth quarters. MBC also brewed three seasonal beers: *Springtide Ale* in March, *Eye of the Hawk Special Ale* from July through October, and *Yuletide Porter* in November and December. [See Exhibit 4-10 for a list of MBC's products].

Although all of the MBC's brands were protected by Federal and California trademark laws, the processes and equipment used to brew its beer were not considered to be proprietary and could not be protected. A licensing agreement with Bridgeport Brewing Co. in Portland, Oregon, prevented Mendocino Brewing from marketing *Blue Heron Pale Ale* in the states of Washington, Oregon, and Idaho.

Bridgeport produced *Blue Heron Bitter Ale* and was likewise prevented from marketing that product throughout the rest of the US.

Awards and Honors

MBC was dedicated to quality graphic design of its packaging as a means to enhance the value of its products. The company's philosophy was that the quality of the package must meet and reflect the quality of what's inside. Nationally-known wildlife artists, including Randy Johnson and Lee Jayred, were retained to design labels and promotional materials.

MBC's products and packaging won several awards. *Eye of the Hawk Select Ale* won the silver medal in the Strong Ale category at the 1990 Great American Beer Festival, a gold medal in 1991, and a bronze medal in 1992. MBC's *Blue Heron Pale Ale* won a bronze medal in the Pale Ale category in 1991. MBC received the Paperboard Packaging Council's Silver Award for Excellence in Packaging and Award for Excellence in Graphic Design and a Northern California Advertising and Design Council's "ADDY" Award for its *Red Tail Ale* packaging in 1990. The design team also won Northern California ADDY award for its new *Blue Heron* label design in 1996.

MBC hoped that its award-winning packaging and point of sale materials would become an even stronger influence, not only on the buying decisions of consumers who faced an increasing number of products, but also on distributors and retailers, who realized the importance of superior package graphic design, making the products easier for the distributor and retailer to promote.

Human Resources

By 1994, MBC had grown to 32 full-time and 33 part-time employees, of which 10 were in management and administration, 19 in brewing operations, and 36 in retail, restaurant, and brewpub operations. By late 1995, when the company had grown to nearly 80 full- and part-time employees, MBC brought in a networked computer system. Management also purchased a sophisticated accounting program but, "we didn't have the time to learn all of its functions," Lovett said. Upon completion of its expansion, MBC hoped to upgrade four employees to full-time status and hire five additional management and administrative employees, three marketing employees and five employees in brewing operations. None of MBC's workforce was unionized. Lovett commented on the company's human resources plans:

> Currently, we are organized by profit center: brewing operations and retail operations. In the next 7–10 years, we may have a "next generation" management team running the company. We are currently grooming that next generation. In the beginning, we [the founders] were self-motivated. A problem is having to motivate new employees. They see it as a job. New employees have to buy into our mission and values, otherwise we won't hire them. Employees have the possibility of becoming owners and we are in the process of accomplishing this. We like to get together and celebrate success.

Mission and Values

MBC was committed to brewing the highest quality beers it could and marketing them profitably, while maintaining high standards of customer service and satisfaction and social responsibility. MBC believed that customers required products with high intrinsic value. It was not sufficient to just have a quality product; a product must distinguish itself from the competition by carrying other values. These values included a commitment to employees, community involvement, and environmental responsibility. An unstated part of MBC's mission was to have the community view it as an asset and as a positive example of how a business should be operated. [See Exhibit 4-11 for MBC's mission statement.]

The venture team instilled these values in employees via weekly team meetings and a monthly newsletter (*The Brewsletter*), using the newsletter to pass along to its customers a commitment to act responsibly. While MBC's strategy was to grow through expanded production and increased wholesale distributions, it promoted its beers as beverages of moderation by producing beers whose distinctive taste and high quality, not quantity, provided customer satisfaction. By adhering to these commitments, the venture team believed that it had captured and could continue to develop a feasible niche in the domestic specialty segment.

Marketing and Distribution

MBC based its marketing strategy on the expectation that demand in the specialty draft market would increase. Historically, the introduction of draft products in restaurants and other establishments had driven bottle sales, which in turn created an increased demand for draft products in areas not serviced. MBC measured customer satisfaction and monitored changing consumer preferences via surveys in its newsletter, *The Brewsletter*, and via interviews with customers, retailers, and distributors. MBC hoped to use survey data to educate and train staff in customer service and satisfaction. According to Lovett:

> We fostered our image by allowing direct interaction between our employees and customers through The Hopland Brewery and through participation in community events and beer festivals. By providing product sampling, information, and education, these direct interaction marketing tools were designed to provide customers with a positive and lasting memory of MBC, which we believed would carry over and influence customers' future buying decisions at retail outlets and restaurants. In 1987, we expanded into the wholesale, distribution market. There wasn't the competition as there is now. It was easier to get the product on the shelf. We had a nice margin at the case level. We watched Fetzer the most as a "marketing company" to get ideas from, in terms of how to price quality beer right. We revise our marketing plan at least once each year.

> Today, our audience includes 21–30 year-olds, trendy, social users, not product educators, not brand loyal, but experimenters. We need to sell them an

"image." We tell them they made the right choice buying this beer. In return, customers will tell us what they want. For example, although we don't have organic growers for suppliers now, we would have to survey customers to "push" for this. Our shareholders are starting to give us ideas, too. In the future, we'll work with shareholders on how to sell and use word-of-mouth advertising more effectively. We also view our shareholders as a source of market intelligence. From what we've heard (from them) recently, we will need to have a WEB page soon.

To accommodate growth, MBC planned to expand its Marketing Department from one (Michael Lovett) to four persons. Lovett's sales and marketing team would initially focus on building relationships with new distributors to gain retail shelf space, next on attracting new customers with a broader line of beers in the Northern California market, and then by identifying and entering potential new regional markets. MBC's wholesale pricing strategy was to position its beers near the top of their segment, which allowed a 25% mark-up with an additional 25% markup by the distributors' retail accounts. MBC believed this strategy was supported by the quality and reputation of its products and could also be sustained by customer demand, so long as demand exceeded current production capacity. Lovett recognized that MBC's wholesale pricing strategy could become more sensitive to downward pressure as direct competitors increased capacity and began to saturate the market with specialty beers. [See Exhibit 4-12 for a table comparing the increases in production capacity by direct competitors.]

Distributors were eager to increase their exposure in the domestic specialty market, as large brewers continued to battle for market share in flat growth segments and as price wars in those segments continued to decrease margins. Laybourn commented:

> Major brewers have determined to take some of this market and they will. "Real" small brewers will have to keep the public aware of who brews what. It will be our job to communicate to our customers the distinction of our products and company. MBC has decided to move quickly to implement a national marketing plan. Market share and profits will not only rely on producing a quality product, but will also require that we find the marketing expertise to design and implement a national marketing plan.

Some large brewers attempted to open distribution channels directly with large retail accounts, using their market power in order to capture higher margins. As a counter-move, MBC initiated a distributor management program. This program entailed understanding the needs of the distributor through market research, surveying current and potential distributors to develop a criteria list and standards of performance, developing comprehensive sales agreements, and maintaining a clear understanding of the standards expected of distributors and standards of brewery support.

Capacity Expansion Plans

In 1992, MBC hired consultants to design and develop a "Master Brewery Plan." MBC then developed an initial expansion plan which provided the basis for its capital budgeting decisions and included budgeted initial costs for the proposed acquisition of equipment and land and facilities construction as well as projected cash flows.

The plan involved the acquisition of a new turn-key brewery along with new fermenting tanks, kegs, packaging and other miscellaneous equipment, all to be installed with the company's existing bottling line at a new 52,000 sq. ft. custom-designed brewing facility to be built on an eight acre parcel of land in Ukiah, CA, approximately 10 miles from the existing brewery. The initial expansion plan called for the purchase of waste water treatment equipment and construction of facilities to house the treatment plant. The new facilities were originally designed and the property and equipment had been chosen to allow for future expansion in several stages. [See Exhibit 4-13 for illustrations of MBC's existing and proposed brewing facilities.]

Net proceeds to MBC from the sale of its Direct Public Offering of shares were estimated to be $3,350,000 after expenses. MBC hoped to use the proceeds over a 12-month period for land ($200,000 for down payment on a $700,000, 8-acre parcel in Ukiah), facilities ($670,000 as down payment on a 52,000 sq. ft. brewery and waste water facility, the balance financed by the Savings Bank of Mendocino County), equipment ($3.9 million to acquire a new turn-key brewery along with new fermenting tanks, kegs, and packaging, water treatment, the balance to be financed by bank loans), and working capital ($339,000) for pre-expansion debt servicing, inventory purchases, accounts payable, or other purposes).

Changeover to the new facility was expected to take place after the new equipment was tested, insuring that no lapse in production would occur. MBC intended to keep The Hopland Brewery online as a channel for developing greater customer interaction, for research and development and test marketing of new specialty brews, and as a possible future brewing education and training site.

Lovett reflected on the fact that, once MBC had succeeded in its capacity expansion efforts, its culture would have to change.

> Our greatest strength is that we got to this growth point. We know the product and the company. Our greatest weakness is that we have no experience in growth processes to take the company to the next level. It's a risk. Shifting from a partnership to a corporation to going public has made us more formalized and structured, and now functional experts have to be hired. We now have a mission, organization chart and objectives, but we will also need to hire management who knows the industry, has marketed new age beverages, knows more than we do and shares our vision that this is an exciting industry. Our vision is to build the Ukiah brewery. In order to do so, we will have to learn government regulations as we grow.

Economic Development Issues

In June 1996, Julie Meier Wright, the Secretary of the California Trade and Commerce Agency, announced that the City of Ukiah Redevelopment Agency has been awarded a loan for $758,000 through California's Rural Economic Development Infrastructure Program (REDIP). In an article in the *Santa Rose Press Democrat*, Wright remarked:

> We live in an ever-changing economy, REDIP gives communities the opportunity to make the changes necessary to bring new industries to these rural areas. Mendocino County will greatly benefit from the expansion of the Mendocino Brewing Company.

The REDIP program provided financing for the construction, improvement or expansion of public infrastructure, with the intent of creating jobs in cities and counties having an unemployment rate either equal to or above the State's average unemployment rate. The City of Ukiah's Redevelopment Agency had applied for funds for an extension of Airport Boulevard, including construction of more than 2,000 feet of road, storm drains and overhead electrical work to the Airport Industrial Park. These improvements were needed to MBC's capacity expansion.

In addition to its capacity expansion, MBC planned to add a total of 24 new jobs by 1997. Due to its heavy reliance on the timber industry for economic growth, Mendocino County had suffered tremendous job losses in recent years. Mendocino County's unemployment rate for April, 1995 was 9.2%, compared to 7.3% for the state.

The Future

MBC's growth strategy was to expand its production capabilities and to increase its wholesale distribution through further penetration of existing and targeted regional markets with a broader line of specialty beers. "We compete primarily on the basis of quality, not price. Quality includes the taste of the products, ingredients, packaging, and the company's image as a responsible member of the community," said Lovett. "As our products become more widely available as the result of the planned capacity expansion, we may be required to compete on the basis of price to a greater extent than we do at present," he continued.

Similarly, the quality of domestic specialty beers being brewed by regional specialty brewers and microbrewers was improving, as many domestic specialty brewers won awards for their beers at competitions here and abroad. Lovett expected that competition at the product quality level would also continue to increase:

> I predict that in 7–10 years, the microbrewery market will become saturated. Shelf space is already dwindling, and there will be consolidations and buy-outs. Brew pubs aren't affected yet. Yes, they'll survive but they won't become large companies. The tradeoff is that we will lose our mystique as we expand, but we'll have to continue to create an "image." The packaging of the company, not just its quality products will be how we—and others— will compete in the future.

Exhibit 4–1   Classification of Breweries

The brewing industry uses the terms of kegs, barrels (bbls.) and cases to measure and sell beer. A keg of beer equals 15.5 gallons, a barrel of beer equals 2 kegs or 31 gallons and a barrel of beer produces 13.8, 24-unit cases of 12-ounce bottles.

A **microbrewery** is defined as a brewery that produces less than 15,000 bbls. of beer per year. Microbreweries typically sell their production via the following methods: 1) the traditional three-tier system (brewer to wholesaler to retailer to consumer); 2) the two-tier system (brewer acting as wholesaler to retailer to consumer); and 3) in some cases, directly to the consumer through carryouts, on-site tap-room or brewery restaurant sales.

A **brewpub** is defined as a restaurant–brewery that brews and sells the majority of its beer on site. Beer is brewed for sale and consumption in an adjacent restaurant and/or bar. Beer is often dispensed directly from a brewery's storage tanks. Where allowed by law, brewpubs often sell beer "to go" and/or distributed products to off-site accounts. When off-site beer sales exceed 50% of total production, then a brewpub can be reclassified as a microbrewery.

A **regional brewery** is defined as having an annual capacity of 15,000 to 500,000 bbls. Although its distribution could be limited in scope to a specific geographical area, for categorization purposes "regional" refers to the brewery's size only.

A **regional specialty brewery** is defined as a regional brewery with its largest-selling brand being a micro or specialty beer.

A **large brewery** typically produces more than 500,000 bbls. annually.

Source: Institute for Brewing Studies, Boulder, CO.

Exhibit 4–2   Recent Initial Public Offerings by Microbreweries

Boston Beer Co. (Boston, MA)	Nation's number one microbrewery; primarily engaged in contract brewing; sold 961,000 barrels in 1995.	Raised $60 million in 1995 DPO; *Samuel Adams* label mainly brewed by Pittsburgh Brewing and Blitz-Weinhard (owned by Stroh).
Buffalo Brewing (Buffalo, NY)	New York's number one microbrewery; ranked the 17th largest microbrewery in the US.	Raised more than $1 million by going public in 1994; proceeds will be used for new product lines and additional equipment.
Hart Brewing (Seattle, WA)	Washington's second largest brewery began as a microbrewery and grew into a regional brewery before going public.	Raised $35 million in December 1995 for capacity and geographical expansion.
Mile High Brewing (Denver, CO)	Venture between Ron Smith founder and CEO of Vail Valley Vintners and Jim Bernau president of Willamette Valley Brewing of Oregon; began brewing in November 1993.	First public microbrewery in Colorado; raised approximately $1.8 million on their first public offering in 1994.
Portland Brewing (Portland, OR)	Founded in 1986 by home brewers Fred Bowman and Art Larrance; later partnered with Robert MacTarnahan, who contributed $2 million in capital.	First microbrewery to go public (1993); have raised nearly $4 million in three offerings.
Red Hook Brewing (Seattle, WA)	Founded in 1981 by Paul Shipman and Gordon Bowker (Starbucks Coffee) as Independent Ale Brewery; long-term, exclusive distribution agreement with Anheuser-Busch (owns 25% stake) in 1994; sales $26 million, net profits of $3.1 million in 1995.	1,956,614 shares of common stock were offered at $17 per share in 1995; proceeds used to build a $30 million, 250,000-barrel brewery in New Hampshire.
Rock Bottom Restaurants (Boulder, CO)	Incorporated April 1993; one of the first brew-restaurants to be publicly traded; operate in Colorado, Minnesota and Texas.	First offering netted approximately $16.5 million in proceeds, mostly used to build new restaurants.
Seattle Brewing Co. (Seattle, WA)	Founded by Jim Bernau; brewery construction began in early 1995.	Raised $2.4 million in their first stock offering (8/94 to build a new microbrewery).
Willamette Valley Brewing (Portland, OR)	Founded by Jim Bernau; company began brewing in November 1993.	Raised $2.4 million on their 1993 IPO and raised an additional $1.2 million on their second offering.

Source: Sonomoa State Univesity Craft Brewing Business Institute.

Exhibit 4-3 Mendocino Brewing Co.—Venture Team Profiles

Michael Laybourn, 58, CEO, President and Director (co-founder and officer since 1982. Prior to MBC, Laybourn co-owned and operated Thunder Road Design and Construction. He is the VP of the California Small Brewers Association and was elected Chairman of the Brewers Association of America in 1995. Laybourn has a B.F.A. from Arizona State University.

Norman Franks, 49, CFO, VP, Treasurer and Director has been an officer since 1982. Prior to MBC, Franks co-owned and operated Thunder Road Design and Construction. He has a B.S. in mechanical engineering from UC Berkeley.

Michael Lovett, 49, Marketing Director, Secretary and Director, joined MBC in 1983 as Assistant Master Brewer and became Marketing Director in 1987. Between 1980–1983, was VP Quality Control of New Albion Brewing Co. From 1976–1980, Lovett was Production Superintendent at Farm Foods in San Francisco. He is Membership Chairman and past Technical Chairman of the Master Brewers Association of the Americas. He has a B.A. in Psychology from San Francisco State College.

Eric G. Bradley, 58, Director, became Director in 1994 and will serve until 1995. Bradley has been a business and financial consultant since 1988. He was employed 20 years with Kaiser Aluminum & Chemical Corp. in positions rising from Division Controller to Business Manager. He is a Fellow of the Institute of Chartered Accountants (UK) and a Certified Personal Financial Planner).

Dan Moldenhauer, 62, Director, is a management consultant. He was president of Conex Products Inc. of Dublin, CA from 1988–1990, a company formed from assets divested by Kaiser Aluminum & Chemical Corp. and later sold to Coleman Cable Systems. Moldenhauer served in several capacities with Kaiser Aluminum from 1971–1988, most recently as president of the subsidiary.

John Scahill, 58, Facilities Manager, has served MBC since its inception. Scahill used to be a self-employed rancher. He has a background in construction and counseling and has a B.S. degree in sociology from UC Berkeley.

Donald Barkley, 43, Master Brewer, joined in 1983. Prior to joining MBC, Barkley was Head Brewer and Plant Manager at New Albion Brewing Co. from 1981 to 1983. Barkley joined New Albion in 1978 and held several positions. He has a BS degree in fermentation science from UC Davis.

SOURCES: Mendocino Brewing Company, 10-K filing, 12/31/95 and direct public offering Prospectus.

Exhibit 4-4 Mendocino Brewing Company—Comparative Income Statements, 1993-1996

| | QUARTERLY REPORT FOR: | | FISCAL YEAR ENDING: | | |
	06/30/96	03/31/96	12/31/95	12/31/94	12/31/93
NET SALES	$1,209,290	$ 631,034	$3,566,500	3,365,600	3,363,908
COST OF GOODS	545,711	324,739	1,846,500	1,840,900	1,786,865
GROSS PROFIT	663,579	306,295	1,720,000	1,524,700	1,577,043
SELL GEN&ADMIN EXP	579,612	429,531	1,537,300	1,324,700	1,375,771
OPERATING PROFIT	83,967	(123,236)	182,700	200,000	201,272
NON-OPERATING INC	(43,274)	11,219	147,600	29,000	25,541
INTEREST EXPENSE	—	—	3,700	4,200	6,088
INCOME BEFORE TAX	40,693	(112,017)	326,600	224,800	220,725
PROV FOR INC TAXES	(21,500)	800	152,900	71,500	0
NET INCOME	$ 62,193	$ (112,817)	$ 173,700	$ 153,300	$ 220,725
OUTSTANDING SHS.	2,322,222	2,322,222	2,322,222	2,220,445	—

Segment data, FY 1995	SALES	OP. INCOME
BREWING OPERATIONS	$2,775,500	$758,400
HOPLAND BREWERY	$ 959,600	$ 34,600

SOURCES: Mendocino Brewing Company, 10-K filing, 12/31/95 and direct public offering Prospectus.

Exhibit 4–5 Mendocino Brewing Company—Comparative Balance Sheets, 1994–1996

| | QUARTERLY REPORT FOR: | | FISCAL YEAR ENDING: | |
	06/30/96	03/31/96	12/31/95	12/31/94\
ASSETS				
CASH	$ 21,226	$ 523,410	$1,696,100	$2,900,800
RECEIVABLES	550,382	250,075	458,900	293,900
INVENTORIES	463,532	448,709	256,200	202,000
NOTES RECEIVABLE	110,088	67,843	—	—
OTHER CURRENT ASSETS	—	—	62,600	25,300
TOTAL CURRENT ASSETS	1,145,228	1,290,037	2,473,800	3,422,000
PROP, PLANT & EQUIP	—	—	3,954,100	301,000
ACCUMULATED DEP	6,947,661	5,197,818	—	—
NET PROP & EQUIP	—	—	3,954,100	301,000
OTHER NON-CUR ASSETS	23,575	14,344	—	—
DEFERRED CHARGES	—	—	15,100	60,500
DEPOSITS, OTHER ASSETS	<u>98,413</u>	<u>94,672</u>	<u>71,000</u>	<u>254,600</u>
TOTAL ASSETS	$8,214,877	$6,596,871	$6,514,000	$4,038,100
LIABILITIES & NET WORTH	06/30/96	03/31/96	12/31/95	12/31/94
NOTES PAYABLE	$ 360,000	$ 400,000	—	—
ACCOUNTS PAYABLE	367,982	138,131	$ 105,700	$ 144,700
CUR LONG TERM DEBT	10,021	8,104	10,400	7,900
ACCRUED EXPENSES	2,532,522	1,164,192	1,364,400	149,800
INCOME TAXES	—	—	34,200	12,400
TOTAL CURRENT LIAB	3,270,525	1,710,427	1,514,700	314,800
DEFERRED CHARGES/INC	20,200	20,200	20,200	—
LONG TERM DEBT	550,652	554,937	554,900	—
TOTAL LIABILITIES	3,841,377	2,285,564	2,089,800	314,800
PREFERRED STOCK	227,600	227,600	227,600	227,600
COMMON STOCK NET	3,869,569	3,869,569	3,869,600	3,342,400
RETAINED EARNINGS	276,331	214,138	327,000	153,300
SHAREHOLDER'S EQUITY	<u>4,373,500</u>	<u>4,311,307</u>	<u>4,424,200</u>	<u>3,723,300</u>
TOT LIAB & NET WORTH	$8,214,877	$6,596,871	$6,514,000	$4,038,100

SOURCES: Mendocino Brewing Company, 10-K filing, 12/31/95 and direct public offering Prospectus.

Exhibit 4–6 Mendocino Brewing Company—Statement of Cash Flows Provided by Operations, 1995

	FYE 12/31/95
CASH PROVIDED BY (USED IN) OPERATIONS	
NET INCOME (LOSS)	$ 173,700
DEPRECIATION/AMORTIZATION	49,300
NET INCREASE (DECREASE) IN ASSETS/LIABILITIES	(237,700)
OTHER ADJUSTMENTS, NET	21,100
NET CASH PROVIDED BY (USED IN) OPERATIONS	$ 6,400
CASH FROM INVESTMENTS	
(INCREASE) DECREASE IN PROPERTY & PLANT	$ (2,922,800)
OTHER CASH INFLOW (OUTFLOW)	(27,800)
NET CASH PROVIDED BY(USED IN) INVESTMENTS	$ (2,950,600)
CASH FLOWS FROM FINANCING	
ISSUANCES (PURCHASES) OF EQUITY SECURITY	$ 568,900
INCREASE (DECREASE) IN BANK, OTHER BORROWINGS	(11,700)
OTHER CASH INFLOW (OUTFLOW)	1,182,300
NET CASH PROVIDED BY (USED IN) FINANCING	$ 1,739,500
NET CHANGE OF CASH/CASH EQUIVALENTS	(1,204,700)
CASH/CASH EQUIVALENTS AT START OF YEAR	2,900,800
CASH/CASH EQUIVALENTS AT YEAR END	$ 1,696,100

SOURCE: Mendocino Brewing Company, 10-K filing, 12/31/95.

Exhibit 4–7 Mendocino Brewing Company—Selected Comparative Financial Ratios, 1993–1995

	FISCAL YEAR ENDING:		
	12/31/95	12/31/94	12/31/93
Current ratio	1.63	10.87	2.63
Quick ratio	1.42	10.15	1.96
Days receivables	46.32	31.44	28.78
Inventory turnover	13.92	16.66	18.93
Times interest earned	89.27	54.52	37.26
Fixed asset turnover	0.90	11.18	16.26
Total asset turnover	0.55	0.83	3.12
Total debt : Total assets	0.32	0.08	0.27
Total debt: Common equity	0.50	0.09	0.38
Sales/Cash	2.10	1.16	11.37
SG&A/Sales	0.43	0.39	0.41
Inventories: Days sales	25.86	21.61	19.02
Net Sales/Working capital	3.72	1.08	7.17
Net income/Net sales	0.05	0.05	0.07
Net income/Total assets	0.03	0.04	0.20
Net income/Invested capital	0.03	0.04	0.28
Net income/Common equity	0.04	0.04	0.28
Net sales/employee	$49,535	$45,481	—

SOURCE: Disclosure On-Line

Exhibit 4–8 Selected Comparative Financial Ratios for Microbreweries

	Ownership	
	Public [n=16]	Private [n=6]
Current	2.58 times	1.76 times
Quick	.88 times	92 times
Days receivables	35.02 days	37.87 days
Inventory turnover	53.02 days	105.19 days
Days payables	53.43 days	64.23 days
Times interest earned	6.80 times	1.82 times
Debt coverage indicator	3.89 times	12.32 times
Assets to equity	.88 times	1.31 times
Liabilities to equity	.43 times	.98 times
Return on equity	5.50%	-8.83%
Return on assets	3.88%	-2.18%
Fixed assets turnover	1.54 times	2.12 times
Total assets turnover	.90 times	.99 times

Source: Sonoma State University Craft Brewing Business Institute survey of microbrewers, Fall 1996.

Exhibit 4-9   Inputs for Malt Beverages

Economic Sector or Industry Providing Inputs	%
Metal cans	31.5
Glass containers	15.8
Malt	7.6
Advertising	7.4
Imports	6.8
Paperboard containers & boxes	3.6
Motor freight	1.7
Miscellaneous crops (rice, barley, wheat, hops)	1.7
Electric services	1.5
Gas production	1.4
Feed grains (corn, sorghum, soy bean)	1.0
Crowns & closures	1.0

Source: US Department of Commerce, *Benchmark Input-Output Accounts for the US Economy*, July 1991.

Exhibit 4-10   Mendocino Brewing Company—Products

Company Product Description.

Red Tail Ale, a full flavored amber ale, is the flagship brand of Mendocino Brewing. It has a long lasting complex character created by a blend of pale and caramel malted barley and balanced to a somewhat dry finish with Yakima Valley whole hops.

Blue Heron Pale Ale is a golden ale, with a full body and a distinctive hop character. Tending toward the "India Pale Ale" style, this ale leaves a fresh, clean hoppy aftertaste. Named for the Great Blue Heron, which has nesting areas in the Hopland area, this ale is made with 100% pale malted barley and Cluster and Cascade hops.

Eye of the Hawk Ale is a high gravity deep amber ale. It is a rich flavored, smooth ale which is brewed in the summer and fall. Caramel and pale malted barley are used. The brew is then balanced with Cluster and Cascade hops to make a very drinkable, strong ale.

Black Hawk Stout is the fullest in flavor and body of the Company's brews. It is a dry, crisp stout with a rich taste achieved by blending fully roasted black malt and caramel malts along with two-row pale malt. It is then balanced with Cluster and Cascade hops.

Yuletide Porter is a deep brown ale made during November and December with 100% malted barley, using pale, caramel, and black malts. With the traditionally rich, creamy flavor balanced with Cluster and Cascade whole hops, the ale has a slightly dry, yet rich finish and a delicate spiciness. *Yuletide Porter* has been a tradition at Mendocino Brewing since 1987.

Peregrine Pale Ale is brewed for a more delicate flavor and character. It is named for the Peregrine Falcon. This ale is a classic golden ale brewed with 100% pale malt and Cascade hops. This ale is featured exclusively at the Hopland Brewery.

Springtide Ale is brewed around St. Patrick's Day and is always an unusually flavored pale ale. The spices vary from year to year and the ale appears as a fresh, flowery, spicy golden ale. It is on tap only at The Hopland Brewery in the springtime.

Exhibit 4–11 Mendocino Brewing Company's Mission Statement

Mission: Our mission is to create distinctive beers of the highest quality we can and market them profitably, realizing that the customer is the number one priority. We have a reputation for high quality natural products, and we believe that the company can continue that tradition, after our initial expansion, by focusing on four areas of production: 1) new modern brewing equipment installed in a custom designed brewing facility; 2) traditional brewing methods, 3) carefully selected ingredients including a unique strain of yeast (we have developed a yeast management program that includes pure culturing and propagation techniques, yeast analysis in our laboratory, continual monitoring of yeast performance and a yeast maintenance plan to ensure yeast viability—we maintain samples of the strain at two offset locations), and 4) brewing experience and expert knowledge along with a passion for brewing high quality beers.

Position: We compete primarily on the basis of quality; therefore, to ensure that our brewing standards are among the highest in the industry, we use carefully selected ingredients, traditional brewing methods, and specially trained craftsmen to brew high quality beers. We use a unique strain of yeast (first introduced in New Albion Brewing Co. in the late 1970s and purchased by the company in 1983 and not commercially available) that produces distinctive tasting beers, and we strive to maintain the fresh quality of our beers after distribution by conducting field sampling and through distributor and retailer education. As part of our initial expansion plan, we intend to acquire new brewing equipment and build a custom-designed brewing facility, both of which, we believe, will increase the consistency and further enhance the quality of our beers as well as make our brewing operations more efficient.

Expansion: We believe that consumer demand already exists for our initial expansion to a production capacity of 50,000 bbls. per year. Working with various consultants, we have developed an initial expansion plan which provided the basis for our capital budgeting decisions. Also, both new equipment and the new facilities have been designed to permit future production capability expansion.

Wholesale Distribution: A factor critical to our post-expansion success and long-term growth is our ability to maintain positive relationships with and attract new distributors and retail outlets. We plan to implement a distributor management program and competitive pricing strategy.

Marketing: Our promotional strategies are designed to create brand awareness and to reinforce a distinct brand image built on quality products, customer service, and social responsibility. We build our product identity and positioning as a leader in the industry by utilizing high quality graphics in its packaging and marketing materials and through our presence at selected promotional events.

Brand Loyalty through Customer Service, Interaction and Satisfaction: We believe that achieving and maintaining brand loyalty not only through product excellence but also through customer service, interaction and satisfaction are primary keys to our success.

Social Responsibility: We strive to be a leader among all businesses in addressing areas of social concern. MBC remains committed to acting in a responsible manner that provides value to our shareholders, customers, employees, the community and the environment.

Source: Mendocino Brewing Company, Direct Public Offering Prospectus.

Exhibit 4-12 Capacity Increases by Competitors in the Microbrewing Segment

Company name	Location	Capacity, thousand bbls.		Annual Growth %
		1992	1993	
Boston Beer Co.	Boston, MA	273	450	65%
Sierra Nevada Brewing Co.	Chico, CA	68	104	53
Anchor Brewing Co.	San Francisco, CA	82	92	11
Pete's Brewing Co.	Palo Alto, CA	36	75	110
Redhook Ale Brewery	Seattle, WA	49	73	49
Widmer Brewing Co.	Portland, OR	28	41	47
Full Sail Brewing Co.	Hood River, OR	29	38	34
Hart Brewing Co.	Kalma, WA	18	32	83
Portland Brewing Co.	Portland, OR	9	17	85
Bridgeport Brewing Co.	Portland, OR	13	16	20
Mendocino Brewing Co.	Hopland, CA	13	13	0

Source: Institute for Brewing Studies, *"1993 Beer and Brewery Statistics, Estimated Total Removals."*

Exhibit 4-13 Mendocino Brewing Company's Proposed Capacity Expansion

The Hopland Brewpub

Architect's rendering of the new Ukiah Brewery

Wire Bender Corp.

Sexual Harassment at Wire Bender Corp. (A)

Sam Brown, Plant Comptroller for Wire Bender Corporation, glanced up to see Teri Whittacker, Human Resource Manager, and Pat Lancaster, Secretary-Treasurer, striding purposefully toward his open door. It was apparent from their expressions as they entered his office that this was no social call.

Lancaster closed the door as Whittacker spoke, "We have a sexual harassment complaint. Jane Troxler, an employee in the wire cutting area, says her supervisor, Fred Swink, has been making sexual advances toward her. She says he makes remarks laced with sexual innuendo and hints that a promotion might be possible for Troxler if she complies with his wishes. Troxler says she asked him to stop, but Swink's advances continue. Troxler has a witness who corroborates her story."

"The president and I would like you to serve on a panel with Teri and Joe Russell, Fred Swink's manager, to investigate the charges," Lancaster said. "We need the panel to report its findings and recommendations as soon as possible. You have the authority to question anyone you think necessary, but careful not to discuss it with anyone outside this investigation, or to accuse anyone of anything before you know the facts. We need your report in no more than a week. Can you do this?"

Company Background

Wire Bender Corporation manufactured products made from steel wire in several small plants located in close proximity in south Georgia. The company had been in business since 1989 and employed 260 workers. Its sales in 1997 exceeded $31 million.

A partial organization chart is shown in Exhibit 5–1. The president performed most of the marketing functions for the firm. Pat Lancaster, as Secretary-Treasurer of the corporation, functioned as the Chief Financial Officer. The Vice President for Manufacturing supervised the six plants each of which had a Plant Manager and two shift supervisors. Accounting and human resource functions for all six plants were centralized. The plant which employed Jane Troxler and Fred Swink produced steel wire shelving like that found in the closets of some residential housing.

Jane operated a mat welder, a machine that welds straight wire rods into a latticework design to form wire shelving. A number of wire rods were placed on a bed parallel to each other and a second layer was placed atop the first layer parallel to each other and perpendicular to the first layer. When Jane tripped the switch, welding heads descended from above and welded the rods together to form wire mesh.

As Shift Supervisor, Fred circulated around the plant monitoring operations and solving problems. He passed Jane's position about every ninety minutes unless he was delayed be a problem in another area. He supervised thirty-seven workers who handled material, operated machines, or performed maintenance; and so had little time for social interaction that was not job related. The close proximity of the workers made it virtually impossible for interactions to occur without being observed by others.

Jane's complaint was not the first sexual harassment charge received by the company. Since the Anita Hill/Clarence Thomas allegations in 1993, Wire Bender has had several. One involved a male plant employee touching a female clerk who worked in the human resource department. Following that incident, the company revised its sexual harassment policy and adopted the one in Exhibit 5–2 in 1995.

The Investigation Panel's First Meeting

Brown agreed to serve with Whittacker and Russell on the panel set up to investigate Troxler's allegations against Swink. The next morning they met to plan their investigation. They started by reviewing the company's sexual harassment policy. Although the policy provided general guidelines, it was not specific enough to guide their investigation. The panel agreed that its first task was to develop an action plan for how to run the investigation. As they began to brainstorm ideas, Brown declared "We must conduct the investigation as thoroughly, as objectively, and as confidentially as possible." The others concurred.

Sexual Harassment at Wire Bender Corp. (B)

Brown, Whittacker, and Russell quickly developed a plan to guide their investigation of Troxler's sexual harassment complaint. Shown in Exhibit 5-3, the plan articulated both the guiding principles of the investigation and the investigators' intended actions.

The next day, the panel began its investigation by questioning Troxler. Troxler described a history of escalating harassment that started with winks and sexually suggestive remarks, and gradually developed into Swink making passes at her and asking her to meet him away from work. According to Troxler, Swink had recently begun to stalk her, following her home at night and to the school where she took night classes. "He said if I played my cards right I could really have it made on my job." She claimed that on a couple of occasions she had been so upset by Swink's behavior that she confided in her boyfriend, Jim Atkins, another Wire Bender employee. Atkins threatened to "get physical" with Swink, but she talked him out of it. The latest incident had occurred only a few days before, when Swink left a note beneath the windshield wiper of Troxler's car—an invitation to meet him at a bar in a town about twenty miles away. Troxler and her co-worker, Becky Hardin, read the note. When Brown asked Troxler if she still had the note, she said she did not. "I tore it up and threw it away. I was afraid my boyfriend would find it and start trouble." When asked how long this problem had been occurring, Troxler replied, "for over a year, but I was too scared to report it." Whittacker reminded her that the company's policy protected her from any sort of retaliation. She said she knew that but was still scared.

Next, the panel interviewed Becky Hardin, Troxler's friend and co-worker, who was with her when Troxler found the note on her windshield. Hardin supported Troxler's story about the note and its contents. She also stated that she had observed a couple of incidents when Swink had made advances toward Troxler at work. Becky said that Troxler declined the advances and that Swink had simply backed away, shrugged his shoulders, and smiled.

After interviewing Hardin, the panel met with Swink. When Russell explained the reason for the meeting, Swink appeared shocked. He insisted repeatedly that he had never made any kind of advance toward Troxler or any other woman. He stated that he always tried to be friendly, yet respectful, to all of his co-workers. In fact, he tried to be mindful of any "off-color" jokes being told to women on the job. He claimed to know nothing of the events of which Troxler had accused him.

Facing conflicting stories from Troxler and Swink, the panel had to decide what to do next. Given that one witness already had supported Troxler's accusations, should they end the investigation now and decide in her favor? Widening the investigation risked violating both parties' confidentiality. If they decided to expand the investigation, who else should they interview? And should they suspend Swink until the investigation was completed?

Sexual Harassment at Wire Bender Corp. (C)

Brown, Whittacker, and Russell agreed that Troxler and Hardin's evidence was compelling but decided that they needed to expand their investigation before making a decision in the case. They had pledged to remain openminded during the investigation, and believed that they should dig deeper to see if they could uncover evidence to support Swink's protestations of innocence. Since Swink had denied Troxler's allegations, they decided not to suspend him from work while the investigation continued, but they did temporarily reassign him to supervise another shift so that he and Troxler would not have to work together. They warned Swink to have no contact with Troxler; to do so could result in immediate suspension or termination. They also asked him not to talk to other employees about this problem until the investigation was resolved.

Interviews with Other Wire Bender Personnel

The panel next interviewed Troxler's boyfriend, Jim Atkins. Atkins did not work with either Troxler or Swink, but was employed in a different Wire Bender plant that was about a mile from the company's administrative facility. Initially the panel had some misgivings about talking with Atkins, but decided that since his testimony could help to corroborate Troxler's story they should interview him. Brown described the interview, "We did not tell him the charges that Troxler had made. We simply asked if she had made any statements about how she liked working for Swink. Atkins laughed and said, "I think she loves working for him, but I've been trying to get her to transfer to another department. She went with him in high school, you know, and I don't think she ever got over him. Personally I wish she didn't work for him. She flirts and doesn't keep her mind on the job sometimes." This was not the response we expected. We expected him to be irate upon hearing Swink's name, in light of what Troxler had said earlier. He never mentioned Swink's harassing Troxler or that he was even aware of it. This part of the puzzle did not fit. Why would he not take the opportunity to inform management of the harassment if he was incensed about it? At that point we were very confused!"

Rather than probing for more information from Atkins, the panel proceeded with the investigation by interviewing eight of Troxler's co-workers. They asked general open-ended questions in an attempt to avoid leading the witnesses. Of the eight employees interviewed, six of them pointed out that there was definitely a harassment problem on the shift, but not the problem about which the panel expected to hear. Troxler's co-workers contended that she frequently made sexually explicit remarks to Swink and vowed that she would "get him back in the sack if it was the last thing she ever did." Swink, on the other hand, ignored the remarks or simply laughed them off. One employee reported that after one of these "brush-offs" Troxler was beside herself with anger.

Second Interviews with Hardin and Troxler

Shortly after interviewing Troxler's co-workers, Becky Hardin sent word to the panel that she wanted to speak to them again. Becky was clearly nervous when she walked into the room. Whittacker told her that the panel had interviewed several other employees and were confused by the conflicting stories she and her co-workers had told. Hardin responded that she had lied for Troxler out of friendship. She said that she had never witnessed Swink harassing Troxler. Troxler and Swink had dated in high school but the relationship went sour; and Swink started dating another girl, who later became his wife. Troxler had never gotten over the breakup.

The panel decided to meet with Troxler and confront her with their findings. When Russell told her that the panel had interviewed her boyfriend, she became very angry and shouted, "What gives you the right to talk to Jim?" Brown asked Troxler why Atkins didn't seem to be aware of Swink harassing her, in conflict with her claim that Atkins was incensed by the harassment. Troxler exploded, "It helped my story sound more believable. Since when are you managers going to take my word over that of a supervisor? But that's OK, because I have a witness." When

Brown told her that Hardin had changed her testimony, Troxler stormed out of the room, slamming the door so hard that the walls shook.

The Panel's Finding

After the scene with Troxler, the panel quickly agreed that her accusations had no merit. They met with Pat Lancaster, the Secretary-Treasurer, and informed him of the outcome. He was as surprised as the panel had been by the unexpected finding. The panel also talked with Swink to inform him of their finding. He seemed rather embarrassed but confirmed Troxler's actions. Brown asked Swink why he had not said anything about Troxler's harassment during or prior to the investigation. Swink replied that he was embarrassed by Troxler's actions and that he would have been the brunt of jokes if he had reported them. When falsely accused by her, he believed that nothing he said would have any bearing on the outcome. "Don't you know that when it comes to sexual harassment, it's always the guy's fault?," Swink ended.

The panel was faced with one last set of decisions—whether and how to discipline Troxler and Hardin for their false allegations against Swink. Although the company's harassment policy provided that any employee found to have engaged in sexual harassment would be disciplined, it did not contain provisions for what to do in cases of false allegations of harassment. Without a clear policy to guide them, Russell, Brown, and Whittacker had to decide whether to discipline either woman, and if so, whether to treat them equally or differently.

Exhibit 5-1 Wire Bender Corporation Organization Chart

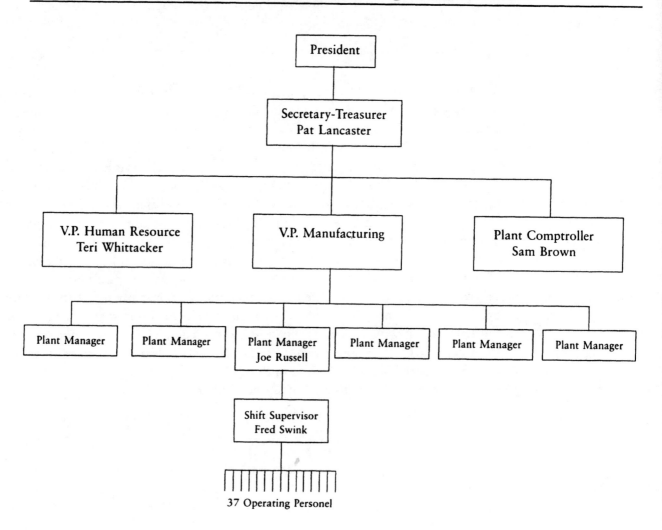

Exhibit 5-2 Wire Bender Corp. Harassment Policy

Harassment   Policy #6.1 Rev 11/95

In order to promote a positive, amiable and pleasant atmosphere in which to work, Wire Bender Corporation is committed to creating and maintaining a workplace that is free from unlawful harassment of any form. This includes, but is not limited to, sexual, racial, religious, gender or sexual orientation forms of harassment. Any form of harassment from one employee toward another will not be tolerated and will be dealt with promptly and thoroughly. Specific policies of harassment follow.

Sexual Harassment

Unwelcome sexual advances, physical or verbal conduct of a sexual nature, and requests for sexual favors all constitute sexual harassment if one or more of the following conditions exist:

A person feels that submission to the unwelcome conduct is necessary in order to obtain or keep their job.

A person feels that decisions of employment such as raises, promotions, etc. depend on whether he or she submits to or rejects the conduct.

The conduct interferes with a person's performance or creates an intimidating, offensive or hostile work environment.

1. Wire Bender Corporation prohibits sexual harassment by <u>all</u> employees; including but not limited to team leaders, supervisors and managers.

2. Our employee's are Wire Bender Corporation's greatest asset. As such, employees have a right to expect an environment free of sexual harassment. Any employees who feel that they have been harassed should inform the Human Resource Manager, or any other manager with whom they feel comfortable discussing the situation, immediately. In cases of harassment, "Chain of Command" rules do not apply. Employees have the right to discuss the matter with any manager they please and may do so without consulting with their team leader, supervisor or manager. Additionally, employees who avail themselves of this right will in no way be disciplined for not following grievance guidelines.

3. Any employee who complains of sexual harassment will not receive any form of retaliation from fellow employees. Retaliation toward an individual filing a sexual harassment complaint will result in severe disciplinary action.

4. When a sexual harassment complaint is received, the team leader, supervisor or manager will immediately inform the Human Resource Manager. The Human Resource Manager will then conduct an investigation of the complaint without delay or the complainant may request a panel to conduct the investigation consisting of the Human Resource and two other impartial managers. The complainant and witnesses, if any, will be interviewed. Should impartiality prove to be a problem that might result in a slanted decision in favor of either party,

either party may request an impartial outside intermediary, paid for by the company.

5. In order to obtain full information regarding a sexual harassment complaint, panel members have the right, at their discretion, to interview any employee of Wire Bender Corporation regarding a sexual harassment complaint.

6. An investigation will be conducted as thoroughly and as discreetly as possible. All information involved in a sexual harassment complaint will be kept strictly confidential by all members of the panel. Panel members are not allowed to discuss information regarding the complaint outside of the other panel members. At no time will any panel member discuss this information with any other employee other than in a formal interviewing process in which that employee may provide further information regarding the complaint. It should be recognized, however, that no investigation can be completely confidential due to the need to question potential witnesses as well as the alleged harasser.

7. Any employee found to have engaged in sexual harassment will be subject to appropriate disciplinary action, up to and including immediate termination from employment without verbal or written warning.

All employees should be aware that both men and women can be harassers or victims of harassment. Additionally, harassment does not have to occur only at work. It can occur at company sponsored events or away from work altogether. A person complaining does not have to be the person that the conduct was directed at. It can be someone else who is affected by the conduct.

Exhibit 5–3 Wire Bender's Sexual Harassment Investigation Panel's Action Plan

a. Conduct the investigation as thoroughly and as confidentially as possible.

b. Avoid making credibility judgments based on the reputation of either person. Remain objective throughout the entire investigation. Never assume that Troxler is being overly sensitive or that Swink is guilty.

c. Phrase questions in a way that will not lead anyone to any kind of conclusion, put words into anyone's mouth, or be accusatory in nature.

d. Talk to Troxler again to gain more insight into the complaint and to obtain further details. This will be crucial when talking to Swink.

e. Talk with the witness without any leading questions and compare her story to Troxler's.

f. Meet with Swink and inform him of the charges that have been filed. Listen to his side of the story. Explain the company's policy. Inform Swink of the investigation's purpose, and when concluded, notify him of the results.

g. If necessary, suspend Swink during the course of the investigation. If evidence supports Troxler's story, Swink will be subject to immediate disciplinary action up to and including termination.

h. Interview other personnel within the department to determine if they have observed or overheard inappropriate incidents.

i. Conduct follow-up interviews with Troxler, Swink, and possibly others, to clear up any misunderstandings or inconsistencies.

j. Meet again in a roundtable discussion reviewing separate notes taken during the interviews, summarizing conclusions, and coming to an agreement on recommendations.

k. Document each step of the investigation and the steps taken to remedy the situation.

l. Meet with Lancaster and present our recommendations.

m. Take immediate action based on the outcome of the investigation.

Bernard's New York Deli

*T*hese deli-bucks are for cash flow what chicken soup is for a cold*, thought Bernard Horowitz as he opened the package the printer had dropped off. Three months earlier he had moved his restaurant, Bernard's New York Deli, to a new location in the upscale Ward Centre shopping area. Faced with needing $30,000 to remodel and buy new equipment, a shortage of cash after the move, and the refusal of his bank to lend more, the deli-bucks were, he sensed, a brilliant inspiration. Customers could buy them for $8 each and after 90 days redeem them to pay for $10 worth of purchases. "Where else could people get 20% on their money in 90 days?" Bernard asked a reporter who had heard about them. If it all worked as planned, he would have the $30,000 cash, the remodeling would be financed, and he'd have a lot of customers coming back.

Background

To build rapport and loyalty with customers, Bernard was advised by a friend in public relations to "tell them your story." He did so by preparing a brochure and placing it at the Deli's entrance. Customers who read it learned that Bernard

By Steven M. Dawson, University of Hawaii. Management cooperated in the field research for this case, which was written solely for the purpose of stimulating student discussion. All events and individuals are real, and some numbers have been changed by request.

Horowitz, namesake but not kin of the legendary pianist, had grown up in the Crown Heights neighborhood of Brooklyn. When he was a kid, he had often followed his nose into the kitchen where his mother chopped, mixed, kneaded, and roasted the family meals. Under her guidance Bernard had learned a thing or two which he'd later put to good use. Bernard's first job, at the age of 13, was as a part-time clerk behind the deli counter of the local food market. "An education like that you don't get in school," he observed later.

In 1974 Bernard went to Hawaii on vacation. Like so many others, before and since, he fell in love with the place. He returned home only to quit his job, pack his things, and move to Hawaii for good. It wasn't long before he was hired to manage Hawaii's first Burger King. Over the next 12 years, he had opened and managed several more and then became the Hawaii district manager. He had learned a lot about food, about managing people and restaurants, and about working for someone else.

In those days whenever he took a trip to the mainland, he had returned with a suitcase of deli food. "There was no other way to get stuff like that in Hawaii in those days," he recalled. Recognizing the need to "nosh," Hebrew for snack, he quit his job at Burger King, took out a second mortgage, and set to work. He used the New York City *Yellow Pages* to locate suppliers to everything from meats (Hebrew National) and gefilte fish (Manischewitz) to soda (Dr. Brown's). In August 1986, "Bernard's New York Deli" opened in a tiny store front near the University. There was room, barely, for table seating for 36 customers. He did take-out business, sold foods not available elsewhere, and acquired a following that craved New York deli specialties. Three years late he moved to suburban Kahala Mall. Room there was even smaller, just seating for 29, but the new location meant he could cater not only to the normal breakfast, lunch, and dinner clientele but also to the late-night movie crowd. "What more could a New Yorker want," Bernard recalled, "than the opportunity to work longer hours?"

A New York Deli in Hawaii?

Hawaii, led by a diverse tourism industry, was a gourmet's delight. Residents and visitors pampered their palates with dishes whose origins evoked the far reaches of the Pacific Rim: kim chee from Korea and sateh from Thailand to local delicacies like poke and poi. In recent years a distinctive new Euro-Asian cuisine developed by Sam Choy, Alan Wong, and Roy Yamaguchi had put Hawaii prominently on the culinary map.

What had been missing in Hawaii for the two centuries since the arrival of Captain James Cook in 1778, and more than a millennium since its first settlement by Polynesian explorers, was a real, Jewish-style deli. It took a malihini, Hawaiian for "newcomer," from Brooklyn to see the opening. When Bernard opened his New York Deli, he brought more than just a "bite of the Big Apple." Most foods in a Jewish-style deli came to New York with immigrants a century ago from the far side of the next ocean, the Atlantic. By bringing a taste of New York, Bernard's actually brought Romania (pastrami), Italy (salami), Germany (sauerkraut and sausage), Ukraine (borscht), and the Baltic (pickled herring and lox).

On the Move, Again

You can't keep a New Yorker away from the Big City for too long, and in January 1997, Bernard closed his suburban deli and moved to Ward Centre, an upscale shopping area located between Waikiki and the downtown business district. The new location had nearly four times the seating—55 seats inside and 66 outside on the lanai. Amused by having a lanai, an outdoor deck, for eating, Bernard wryly observed that not everything had to be like Brooklyn. Colorful pictures, Jewish sayings, street signs from New York, copies of the *New York Times* for sales, and an authentic deli food counter provided the ambience of a New York place-to-be for the action. Parking was ample, and business picked up quickly. Thanks to loyal customers and a feature story in the Sunday newspaper's restaurant section, opening day on January 3 was a big success, and revenues were all Bernard had hoped for. Sales for all of January were $110,000 followed by $100,000 and $105,000 in February and March. Bernard expected that with the existing table setup, sales would average about $95,000 a month.

Good as it was, it could be better. To take full advantage of the new location, the deli needed a little more equipment and a bit of remodeling to increase seating by another 50 customers. In a new small sit-down cafe section, he planned to sell Brooklyn Beer, an exclusive microbrewery label. "This remodeling will really give us a boost," said Bernard, and he expected a 30% increase in sales. Based on the first three months at the new location, and his experience earlier, he expected monthly sales to be as follows:

	Forecast		Forecast
April	$90,00	November	$100,000
May	95,000	December	140,000
June	115,000	January	140,000
July	125,000	February	125,000
August	135,000	March	130,000
September	120,000	April	115,000
October	110,000	May	120,000

In June, sales would be 15 percent higher than without the remodeling, and starting in July the increase would be 30 percent.

The bigger-size restaurant at War Centre meant the action behind the counter could be as frenetic as in a New York eatery. It also meant Bernard had a bigger task of managing the finances. Long gone were the days when he had just three other employees besides himself. At Ward Centre, Bernard started with a staff of 30 servers, preparers, and cleanup people, and it would grow to 42 with the expansion.

The two big expenses in the restaurant were food and labor. Bernard priced items so that the food expenses were about 30 percent of revenues. He trained his wait staff to be careful about needlessly wasting food. One time he pointed to four unused butter slices left on a table. "Each costs us five cents and if this happens ten times a day, seven days a week, by the end of a year we've wasted over $700."

Provide good service, we need repeat customers, but watch the waste was the message.

Employee labor costs were also about 30 percent of revenues and were of two kinds: those he paid directly as wages to employees, and those he paid elsewhere. Hawaii was a tough place to do business when you had high labor costs, thanks to a state government and business environment that a *Forbes* magazine article had called the "New Socialist Republic of Hawaii." With the last paychecks, Bernard had given all his workers two reports: first, the dollars he had paid them as wages and, second, the dollars he had to pay others for them. For a $1,000 monthly wage payment to an employee, he calculated he paid an additional $277.50 as follows:

$76.50	Employer social security withholding
6.50	State temporary disability insurance
61.00	State worker's compensation
115.00	Employer share of mandatory state medical insurance
14.50	State unemployment insurance
4.00	Federal unemployment tax

With three months at the new location and ten years of operating experience, Bernard had a comfortable feel for the relationship of revenues and expenses and did not expect a big change to occur after the remodeling was complete. "You need both more food and more employees when you have a bigger operation." Looking at the big picture and for the range of volume of business he expected to do, food and personnel costs would each be about 30 percent of revenues. Monthly rent at the Centre was $1,500 plus 6 percent of revenues. Other premise expenses, including security, insurance, and utilities, would run about $4,000 plus 6 percent of revenue. Kitchen, dining, and office expenses were 5.5 percent. Selling expenses, including advertising, the 4 percent state excise tax, 1.2 percent credit card charges, and printing, averaged 10.5 percent of revenues. Depreciation averaged $1,500 now and would rise to $2,000 a month in July when the expansion was done. It roughly equaled outlays for new or replacement equipment. Monthly payments on the bank loan were $3,210. All except the food and rent expenses were paid during the month incurred. Food generally had net 30 day terms with no discounts for early payment. Bernard didn't pay himself a regular salary. The Deli was organized as a Subchapter S corporation, and when surplus cash was available at the end of the month above the $5,000 he thought was a comfortable minimum, he took it out. "If my good wife didn't have a job, there'd be some really tough times."

The remodeling and expansion would cost about $30,000, and this was a problem. The move and startup had absorbed all the available funds. Cash was tight, just $3,000 at the start of April, and the outlook for getting more funds was discouraging. April and May usually were slow months for restaurants in Hawaii. Bernard believed it was a combination of the seasonal tourism slowdown and the preoccupation of customers with making tax payments. This meant internal funds would not supply the needed expansion capital and, to make it worse, near-term revenue projections wouldn't look good to the bank. Bernard already had a $160,000 bank loan at an interest rate of 10.75 percent. When he discussed increasing the loan, his loan officer replied, "Not at this time. You're maxed out until we see how the new location goes." Bernard wasn't surprised. "The banks in Hawaii, just like the state authorities, are not pro small business."

Deli-Bucks

Bernard's solution to the shortage of funds came from the gift certificates he'd sold at his very first location to help him get started. Why not use them again, but modified so they could fund the remodeling? Ordinary gift certificates could be redeemed right away and therefore would not fill the bill because the money was needed first for remodeling. The solution: deli-bucks. He'd sell deli-bucks with a 90-day delay before they could be redeemed and a one-year life from date of purchase. Ninety days didn't seem unreasonably long and that would give him time to get the remodeling done. Any longer and it might seem too long to customers. The one-year limit would keep the redemption from dragging out forever.

Customers obviously wouldn't see much sense in paying now instead of paying later. They needed an incentive and a discount would do it. Playing with the numbers, Bernard decided on selling $10 deli-bucks for $8. Ten dollars was a reasonable size for an order, putting out $8 was not a big outlay, and a 20 percent discount seemed enough to offer something of value to customers. With the 30 percent food cost, he felt he had a lot of room to maneuver in giving a discount for early purchase. Whether the deli-bucks were more costly than other sources of funds, such as the bank loan if it had been available, was a question Bernard didn't take time to consider. After all, customers would redeem the certificates for food, not cash. A bank loan in contrast would require a cash repayment. How soon after 90 days the certificates would be redeemed was tough to forecast. Based on his earlier experience with gift certificates, Bernard figured it would take him about three months to sell all the deli-bucks, with 50 percent being sold in April, the first month; 30 percent the second; and 20 percent the third. At this rate, cash collections would approximately match remodeling payments. In accounting terms the deli-buck receipts would be placed in a "precollected revenue" account, with the impact on rent, the state excise tax, and other expenses, except for credit card charges, occurring at redemption. Redemptions would begin in month four and would be at the rate of 50 percent the first eligible month, 10 percent the next, and then 5 percent per month for the remaining seven months of the year. The remaining 5 percent would probably be lost, forgotten, or even kept as souvenirs. For deli-bucks sold in April, 50 percent would thus be redeemed in July, 10 percent in August, and so on. Bernard guessed that 75 percent of the deli-bucks would be redeemed by regular customers and 20 percent by customers who would not otherwise have come to the restaurant. Furthermore, 45 percent of the deli-bucks would be redeemed by regular customers who increased their purchases by an average of $2. Not having to pay for the first $10 would make it tempting to take an extra bagel home, to get a more expensive sandwich, or to splurge on dessert. He'd seen this happen earlier with the gift certificates.

Designing the deli-bucks was easy and a good opportunity to mix marketing with finance. Made to look like oversized currency, the certificates on one side had Bernard's picture, a fancy border with $10 signs in the corners, and the notation that the purchase cost was $8 and the value was $10 in food purchases with no redemption for cash. The other side had the logo for Bernard's New York Deli, a bright red apple with a bite taken out, more $10 signs, and the message "Pay now . . . eat later. These deli-bucks will be used to further our expansion and purchase additional equipment and more seating to make your experience more enjoyable. You will in turn receive a 20% discount on your future purchases." Each certificate had its own serial number so it could be tracked and to discourage counterfeiting.

After hearing about the deli-bucks, Joann Kapololu, manager of the Waikiki Beachcomber restaurant, praised Bernard's idea. "He obviously has a passion for what he does, and came up with something very creative. This brings dollars into his business, allows him to finance his dream, and the people who enjoy his food will be all over it."

The certificate package from the printer held enough of the deli-bucks to raise $30,000, and Bernard prepared an attractive poster to be placed near the restaurant entrance telling customers about them. The wait staff was briefed to respond favorably when customers asked about the certificates. All was ready.

Exhibit 6-1 Cash Budget With Deli bucks

	April	May	June	July	August	September	October	November	December	January	February	March	April	May
Cash inflows														
Revenues	90000	95000	115000	125000	135000	120000	110000	100000	140000	140000	125000	130000	115000	120000
Plus deli bucks	15000	9000	6000	0	0	0	0	0	0	0	0	0	0	0
Less redemptions	0	0	0	-9375	-7500	-5813	-2250	-1875	-1875	-1875	-1875	-1875	-938	-375
Total cash inflows	105000	104000	121000	115625	127500	114188	107750	98125	138125	138125	123125	128125	114063	119625
Cash outflows														
Food	31500	27000	28500	34500	37500	40500	36000	33000	30000	42000	42000	37500	39000	34500
Personnel	27000	28500	34500	37500	40500	36000	33000	30000	42000	42000	37500	39000	34500	36000
Rent	7275	6450	6725	7825	8375	8925	8100	7550	7000	9200	9200	8375	8650	7825
Premises	9400	9700	10900	11500	12100	11200	10600	10000	12400	12400	11500	11800	10900	11200
Kitchen, dining, office	4950	5225	6325	6875	7425	6800	6050	5500	7700	7700	6875	7150	6325	6600
Selling	9630	10083	12147	13013	14085	12530	11523	10478	14678	14678	13103	13628	12064	12596
Depreciation/outlays	1500	1500	1500	2000	2000	2000	2000	2000	2000	2000	2000	2000	2000	2000
Bank loan	3210	3210	3210	3210	3210	3210	3210	3210	3210	3210	3210	3210	3210	3210
Remodeling	15000	9000	6000	0	0	0	0	0	0	0	0	0	0	0
Total cash outlays	109465	100668	109807	116423	125195	120965	110483	101738	118988	133188	125388	122663	116649	113931
Starting cash without withdrawals	3000	-1465	1867	13060	12263	14568	7790	5057	1444	20582	25519	23257	28719	26133
Plus inflows	105000	104000	121000	115625	127500	114188	107750	98125	138125	138125	123125	128125	114063	119625
Minus outflows	-109465	-100668	-109807	-116423	-125195	-120965	-110483	-101738	-118988	-133188	-125388	-122663	-116649	-113931
Net monthly cash flow	-4465	3332	11193	-798	2305	-6778	-2733	-3613	19138	4938	-2263	5463	-2586	5695
Ending cash	-1465	1867	13060	12263	14568	7790	5057	1444	20582	25519	23257	28719	26133	31828
Target cash	5000	5000	5000	5000	5000	5000	5000	5000	5000	5000	5000	5000	5000	5000
Cumulative withdrawals	0	0	8060	8060	9568	9568	9568	9568	15582	20519	20519	23719	23719	26828
Starting cash with monthly withdrawals	3000	-1465	1867	5000	4203	5000	-1778	-4511	-8123	5000	5000	2738	5000	2414
Plus inflows	105000	104000	121000	115625	127500	114188	107750	98125	138125	138125	123125	128125	114063	119625
Minus outflows	-109465	-100668	-109807	-116423	-125195	-120965	-110483	-101738	-118988	-133188	-125388	-122663	-116649	-113931
Net monthly cash flow	-4465	3332	11193	-798	2305	-6778	-2733	-3613	19138	4938	-2263	5463	-2586	5695
Ending cash	-1465	1867	13060	4203	6508	-1778	-4511	-8123	11014	9938	2738	8200	2414	8108
Target cash	5000	5000	5000	5000	5000	5000	5000	5000	5000	5000	5000	5000	5000	5000
Withdrawals	0	0	8060	0	1508	0	0	0	6014	4938	0	3200	0	3108
End cash after withdrawal	-1465	1867	5000	4203	5000	-1778	-4511	-8123	5000	5000	2738	5000	2414	5000

Exhibit 6-2 Cash Budget Without Deli bucks

	April	May	June	July	August	September	October	November	December	January	February	March	April	May
Cash inflows														
Revenue forecast	90000	95000	115000	125000	135000	120000	110000	100000	140000	140000	125000	130000	115000	120000
Less expansion correction	0	0	-15000	-28846	-31154	-27692	-25385	-23077	-32308	-32308	-28846	-30000	-26538	-27692
Total inflows	90000	95000	100000	96154	103846	92308	84615	76923	107692	107692	96154	100000	88462	92308
Cash outflows														
Food	31500	27000	28500	30000	28846	31154	27692	25385	23077	32308	32308	28846	30000	26538
Personnel	27000	28500	30000	28846	31154	27692	25385	23077	32308	32308	28846	30000	26538	27692
Rent	7275	6450	6725	7000	6788	7212	6577	6154	5731	7423	7423	6788	7000	6365
Premises	9400	9700	10000	9769	10231	9538	9077	8615	10462	10462	9769	10000	9308	9538
Kitchen, dining, office	4950	5225	5500	5288	5712	5077	4654	4231	5923	5923	5288	5500	4865	5077
Selling	9450	9975	10500	10096	10904	9692	8885	8077	11308	11308	10096	10500	9288	9692
Depreciation/outlays	1500	1500	1500	1500	1500	1500	1500	1500	1500	1500	1500	1500	1500	1500
Bank loan	3210	3210	3210	3210	3210	3210	3210	3210	3210	3210	3210	3210	3210	3210
Remodeling	0	0	0	0	0	0	0	0	0	0	0	0	0	0
Total cash outlays	94285	91560	95935	95710	98345	95075	86979	80248	93518	104441	98441	96345	91710	89614
Starting cash without withdrawals	3000	-1285	2155	6220	6664	12165	9398	7034	3708	17883	21135	18848	22503	19255
Plus inflows	90000	95000	100000	96154	103846	92308	84615	76923	107692	107692	96154	100000	88462	92308
Minus outflows	-94285	-91560	-95935	-95710	-98345	-95075	-86979	-80248	-93518	-104441	-98441	-96345	-91710	-89614
Net monthly cash flow	-4285	3440	4065	444	5502	-2768	-2364	-3325	14175	3252	-2287	3655	-3248	2694
Ending cash	-1285	2155	6220	6664	12165	9398	7034	3708	17883	21135	18848	22503	19255	21948
Target cash	5000	5000	5000	5000	5000	5000	5000	5000	5000	5000	5000	5000	5000	5000
Cumulative withdrawals	0	0	1220	1664	7165	7165	7165	7165	12883	16135	16135	17503	17503	17503
Starting cash with monthly withdrawals	3000	-1285	2155	5000	5000	5000	5000	-132	-3457	5000	5000	2713	5000	1752
Plus inflows	90000	95000	100000	96154	103846	92308	84615	76923	107692	107692	96154	100000	88462	92308
Minus outflows	-94285	-91560	-95935	-95710	-98345	-95075	-86979	-80248	-93518	-104441	-98441	-96345	-91710	-89614
Net monthly cash flow	-4285	3440	4065	444	5502	-2768	-2364	-3325	14175	3252	-2287	3655	-3248	2694
Ending cash	-1285	2155	6220	5444	10502	2232	-132	-3457	10718	8252	2713	6368	1752	4445
Target cash	5000	5000	5000	5000	5000	5000	5000	5000	5000	5000	5000	5000	5000	5000
Withdrawals	0	0	1220	444	5502	2232	0	0	5718	3252	0	1368	0	0
End cash after withdrawal	-1285	2155	5000	5000	5000	2232	-132	-3457	5000	5000	2713	5000	1752	4445

Exhibit 6-3 First Sensitivity Analysis: Faster Redemption of Delibucks

	April	May	June	July	August	September	October	November	December	January	February	March	April	May
Cash inflows														
Revenues	90000	95000	115000	125000	135000	120000	110000	100000	140000	140000	125000	130000	115000	120000
Plus Deli bucks	15000	9000	6000	0	0	0	0	0	0	0	0	0	0	0
Less redemptions	0	0	0	-15000	-11813	-7688	-1125	0	0	0	0	0	0	0
Total cash inflows	105000	104000	121000	110000	123188	112313	108875	100000	140000	140000	125000	130000	115000	120000
Cash outflows														
Food	31500	27000	28500	34500	37500	40500	36000	33000	30000	42000	42000	37500	39000	34500
Personnel	27000	28500	34500	37500	40500	36000	33000	30000	42000	42000	37500	39000	34500	36000
Rent	7275	6450	6725	7825	8375	8925	8100	7550	7000	9200	9200	8375	8650	7825
Premises	9400	9700	10900	11500	12100	11200	10600	10000	12400	12400	11500	11800	10900	11200
Kitchen, dining, office	4950	5225	6325	6875	7425	6600	6050	5500	7700	7700	6875	7150	6325	6600
Selling	9630	10083	12147	12945	14033	12508	11537	10500	14700	14700	13125	13650	12075	12600
Depreciation/outlays	1500	1500	1500	2000	2000	2000	2000	2000	2000	2000	2000	2000	2000	2000
Bank loan	3210	3210	3210	3210	3210	3210	3210	3210	3210	3210	3210	3210	3210	3210
Remodeling	15000	9000	6000	0	0	0	0	0	0	0	0	0	0	0
Total	109465	100668	109807	116355	125143	120943	110497	101760	119010	133210	125410	122685	116660	113935
Starting cash without withdrawals	3000	-1465	1867	13060	6705	4749	-3881	-5503	-7263	13728	20518	20108	27423	25763
Plus inflows	105000	104000	121000	110000	123188	112313	108875	100000	140000	140000	125000	130000	115000	120000
Minus outflows	-109465	-100668	-109807	-116355	-125143	-120943	-110497	-101760	-119010	-133210	-125410	-122685	-116660	-113935
Net monthly cash flow	-4465	3332	11193	-6355	-1956	-8630	-1622	-1760	20990	6790	-410	7315	-1660	6065
Ending cash	-1465	1867	13060	6705	4749	-3881	-5503	-7263	13728	20518	20108	27423	25763	31828
Target cash	5000	5000	5000	5000	5000	5000	5000	5000	5000	5000	5000	5000	5000	5000
Cumulative withdrawals	0	0	8060	8060	8060	8060	8060	8060	8728	15518	15518	22423	22423	26828
Starting cash with withdrawals	3000	-1465	1867	5000	-1355	-3311	-11941	-13563	-15323	5000	5000	4590	5000	3340
Plus inflows	105000	104000	121000	110000	123188	112313	108875	100000	140000	140000	125000	130000	115000	120000
Minus outflows	-109465	-100668	-109807	-116355	-125143	-120943	-110497	-101760	-119010	-133210	-125410	-122685	-116660	-113935
Net monthly cash flow	-4465	3332	11193	-6355	-1956	-8630	-1622	-1760	20990	6790	-410	7315	-1660	6065
Ending cash	-1465	1867	13060	-1355	-3311	-11941	-13563	-15323	5668	11790	4590	11905	3340	9405
Target cash	5000	5000	5000	5000	5000	5000	5000	5000	5000	5000	5000	5000	5000	5000
Withdrawals	0	0	8060	0	0	0	0	0	668	6790	0	6905	0	4405
After withdrawals	-1465	1867	5000	-1355	-3311	-11941	-13563	-15323	5000	5000	4590	5000	3340	5000
Cumulative withdrawals	0	2552	15893	17013	21360	21360	21360	21360	33427	40114	40114	46147	46147	51838
Starting cash with withdrawals	3000	2855	5000	5000	5000	5000	-810	-2523	-5241	5000	5000	3768	5000	3319
Plus inflows	114000	113500	132500	128125	141000	126188	118750	108125	152125	152125	135625	141125	125563	131625
Minus outflows	-114145	-108803	-119160	-127005	-136653	-131998	-120463	-110843	-129818	-145438	-136858	-133860	-127244	-124253
Net monthly cash flow	-145	4697	13341	1120	4348	-5810	-1713	-2717	22308	6688	-1233	7265	-1681	7372
Ending cash	2855	7552	18341	6120	9348	-810	-2523	-5241	17067	11688	3768	11033	3319	10691
Target cash	5000	5000	5000	5000	5000	5000	5000	5000	5000	5000	5000	5000	5000	5000
Withdrawals	0	2552	13341	1120	4348	0	0	0	12067	6688	0	6033	0	5691
Cash after withdrawals	2855	5000	5000	5000	5000	-810	-2523	-5241	5000	5000	3768	5000	3319	5000

CeeBee's Furniture Outlet: A Case in Strategic Management of a Small Business

Ronald Earl, Sam Houston State University
    mkt_rle@shsu.edu
Olga Thomas, Sam Houston State University
Joe Kavanaugh, Sam Houston State University
    mgt_jkk@shsu.edu
Paul Reed, Sam Houston State University
    mgt_prr@shsu.edu

Case Description

The primary subject matter of this case concerns making strategic management decisions in the context of a small retail business. Key strategic areas that need to be addressed are the *focus of the organization*, and *organizing and staffing the business*. Secondary issues examined include marketing issues such as the right product mix, the right amount of advertising and promotion and the right credit policies. The case has a difficult level of three or four (appropriate for junior or senior level courses). The case is designed to be taught in approximately one class hour and should require no more than three hours of student preparation.

Case Synopsis

CeeBee's is an independently operated discounter of furniture and appliances located in Huntsville, Texas. In business almost three years, it has yet to generate a profit. Typical of many small businesses, the operating owner of CeeBee's is currently "all things to all people," attempting to perform too many diverse functions, and as a consequence has lost focus on the strategic growth of the business. Questions must be answered as how to recapture focus, appropriately organize and staff the business, and build operating infrastructure which will be able to support the business as it prepares to move to the next level. The immediate crises the owner faces are a growing burden of receivables, inefficient management practices, and significant understaffing.

Introduction

As Tom reviews his daily agenda, he looks out at the merchandise from his office in the center of his discount furniture store showroom. To the right of Tom is his accounts receivable bulletin board. Tom posts his delinquent accounts on note cards in one of three columns: zero to thirty days, thirty to sixty days or sixty to ninety days. Tom is concerned about the growing number of note cards in his sixty to ninety day column.

Tom's store has experienced steady growth and is faced with many uncertainties. The following questions race across Tom's mind as he contemplates the store's future. Should the store be expanded to include other product lines such as wide screen televisions? Should CeeBee's open another store in a nearby city? If so, will it be wise to borrow the money necessary for expansion? Would revising or changing the no credit check policy hurt the store financially? How can the new computer be used to improve store operations?

History

On February 20, of 1995, Thomas Churin and Carl Brandon opened CeeBee's Furniture Outlet in Huntsville, Texas. The name CeeBee's came from a combination of the partners' last names. The partners chose Huntsville as a location after looking at several other Texas cities. The main reason for their choice was the low unemployment rate in Huntsville and CeeBee's practice of using verifiable employment as credit for in house financing.

Tom and Carl had been small business owners prior to opening the store. In fact, Tom had a similar discount furniture store in El Campo, Texas. Both men were aware of the elements necessary to be profitable in the discount furniture store business. Tom is the active partner while Carl mainly provides financial support. CeeBee's began as a discount furniture retailer and later expanded the inventory to include appliances.

Local Area

CeeBee's primary market is Huntsville and the counties located within a twenty mile radius. Huntsville is the home of Sam Houston State University and the headquarters of the Texas Department of Criminal Justice (TDCJ) with four prison units within its city limits. Another maximum security prison is now under construction. TDCJ and University employees make up a large portion of the labor force. The population in 1996 was 56,400 people, which included TDCJ inmates and college students residing in Huntsville. The population has a current unemployment rate of 2.5%. In 1996, 45.5% of the labor force earned salaries that were under $19,999 dollars, 23% earned between $20,000–$34,999, 15% earned between $35,000–$49,999, and 16.5% earned $50,000 and over.

Since 1991, Huntsville has experienced 6.59% growth in the number of households. The addition of new apartment complexes and new college students each year, provides a strong market for discount furniture in the community (see Exhibit 7-1).

The downside of the Huntsville community is that it is very close knit. Often, community members are more supportive of local business men and neither Tom nor his partner are originally from Huntsville. However, CeeBee's sponsors community organizations like the youth rodeo and boys baseball. CeeBee's is also a member of the Chamber of Commerce.

External Environment

Competition. There are are six furniture dealers and three furniture rental stores in town. However, only two of these dealers carry the same discount priced furniture product as CeeBee's.

Tom faces competition directly from William's Furniture & Gift Shop located across town from CeeBee's. William's Furniture is a family owned and operated establishment that has served Huntsville for approximately three years and also has a location in Conroe, Texas. William's offers its customers variety, options to customize, and lifetime guarantees on all furniture. William's is well known among the community members and college students for the salesmen's willingness to bargain and an atmosphere of high pressure sales. The average price of a sofa at William's is $650 and the price of a mattress is $399. William's estimates that his turnover is three weeks. Like CeeBee's, William's targets TDCJ employees.

The next closest competitor is Adam's Furniture which is located downtown on the square. Adam's has served the Huntsville community for over 25 years and has a large diversified customer base. Approximately one hundred people enter Adam's daily. It is well known for personalized service and a good reputation. Adam's offers low credit requirements and in-store financing like CeeBee's and Williams. Adam's sells all household furnishing including both furniture and appliances like CeeBee's. It carries name brand products and charges slightly higher prices than both CeeBee's and William's. The average price of a sofa at Adam's is $950.

Exhibit 7 – 1   Huntsville and Walker County Economic Indicator

★Employment	Walker Co. Sep - 97	Texas Sep - 97	U.S. Sep - 97	Walker Co. Sep - 96	Texas Sep - 96	U.S. Sep - 96
Total Labor Force	22,998	9,996,200	137,459,000	22,685	9,810,100	135,011,000
Total Employed	22,433	9,462,000	130,865,000	22,038	9,272,500	128,143,000
Total Unemployed	565	534,200	6,594,000	647	537,600	6,868,000
Percent Unemployed	2.5%	5.3%	4.8%	2.9%	5.5%	5.1%

☆Huntsville Building Permit Values	Oct - 97	Oct - 96	% Variance	1997 YTD	1996 YTD	% Variance
New Residential	$292,000	$669,349	-56.4%	$10,950,430	$16,370,507	-33.1%
New Non-Residential	$0	$341,000	-100.0%	$730,479	$4,489,515	-83.7%
Additions/Renovations	$26,300	$15,250	72.5%	$2,193,877	$3,089,736	-29.0%
Other	$49,875	$50,550	-1.3%	$2,849,152	$363,703	$683.4%
TOTAL	$368,175	$1,076,149	-65.8%	$16,723,938	$24,313,461	-31.2%

◐Walker County Sales Tax Payments	Oct - 97	Oct - 96	% Change	1997 YTD	1996 YTD	% Change
Huntsville (1.5%)	$268,185	$260,088	3.1%	$3,043,661	$2,869,220	6.1%
New Waverly (1.0%)	$3,104	$3,279	-5.3%	$49,082	$37,905	29.5%
Riverside (1.5%)	$3,874	$3,230	19.9%	$37,624	$34,302	9.7%
Walker County (0.5%)	$108,004	$94,197	14.7%	$1,131,069	$1,021,123	10.8%
TOTAL	$383,167	$360,794	6.2%	$4,261,436	$3,962,550	7.5%

Sources
★Employment: Texas Workforce Commission
☆Bldg. Prmt. Valuations: City of Huntsville (YTD Permits are cumulative totals)
◐Sales Tax Payments: Texas Comptroller of Public Accounts Window on State Government Web Site (http://
                                    www.window.texas.gov)
★Miscellaneous: ?? = Calculation cannot be done

Internal Environment

Location. CeeBee's is located in a small business strip shopping center. The store is visible from Highway 75, a heavily traveled road. This highway contains a large majority of Huntsville's family owned small businesses including carpet and antique stores. CeeBee's has a small sign in front of the store and paintings of furniture on the windows. Also, there is always a display in the showcase window. The store has 5000 square feet comprised of a 3750 square foot showroom and office space and a warehouse in back that Tom uses as a repair shop and an area to receive inventory. CeeBee's has adequate parking and is readily accessible from the highway. Tom likes his location and has expressed interest in buying the building.

Management. Tom believes in the principles of hard work and discipline. Her served in the U.S. Navy for four years in Vietnam. After leaving the Navy, Tom worked in construction and traveled extensively for many years. When he returned to the U.S., Tom wanted to utilize his qualities to run his own successful small business. He entered the furniture sales business approximately four years ago and has been working faithfully toward his goal of success ever since.

Tom and Carl are considering opening a second location in a nearby city. They have been researching potential cities but, have not yet found a good location. They anticipate that it will take approximately three years to plan this venture.

Recently, Tom and his wife, Pam, opened a Massage Therapy Service located behind CeeBee's. Pam is a licensed therapist and handles most of the operations for the new business.

Personnel. CeeBee's has one part-time employee Brenda, who mainly works Tuesdays, Thursdays and Saturdays. She is a Sam Houston State University student and has been at CeeBee's since it opened. Brenda is the only person who can run the store in Tom's absence. She will be graduating soon. Eventually, Tom plans to have his wife Pam, work as a part-time employee. Pam is currently enrolled in computer courses at SHSU, she plans to use these skills in both businesses. On occasion Carl comes in from out of town and works in the store. Also, CeeBee's uses an outside CPA firm to handle year end audit and filing of federal and state income tax.

Operations. Tom does all of the bookkeeping for the company by hand, including financial statements, customer billing information and receipts. He also does a monthly physical count of the inventory. Currently, he uses twenty different handwritten spreadsheets for his inventory tracking. Tom also purchases all the store's inventory at market in Houston on Tuesday or Thursday when his assistant works. On average, he makes one trip to Houston per week. Tom normally keeps a low level of inventory on hand to reduce expenses and for tax purposes. The county assesses property tax on a business's inventory and equipment on hand.

Tom estimates that he has approximately 146 customers and record keeping and billing can take a large portion of the month to complete. Recently, Tom purchased a Pentium based Hewlett Packard computer with monitor and a desk jet printer but, he has not learned to use it yet. His wife, Pam, is taking some computer classes and later plans to become responsible for CeeBee's record keeping.

Showroom. The store is busiest early in the month because the majority of customers are TDCJ employees who get paid on the first of the month. CeeBee's has a good repeat business, largely due to Tom's determination to maintain close customer relationships.

CeeBee's carries various discount brands of bedroom and living room sets, mattresses and appliances including refrigerators, microwaves, deep freezers and stoves. The store has some variety merchandise like figurines, rugs, jewelry and a pool table. As an added service, CeeBee's allows customers to order furniture that is not in the store from a catalog. The customer can also choose from over 150 fabrics. The best selling items in the store are living room sets and mattresses. The majority of the merchandise has an average markup of seventy-five percent.

Tom is proud of his store and takes pride in its appearance, and he keeps the showroom very neat and organized. There is a small work area in the showroom that Tom uses to assemble products. The merchandise is arranged in a decorative, spacious manner as opposed to the crowded showroom displays of his competitors. As result, CeeBee's customers can easily browse the store and inspect the merchandise.

Tom does not believe in high pressure sales. When a customer enters, Tom and his assistant let the customer browse the store freely before approaching them. After a sale, Tom prefers that the customer arrange for the delivery of the furniture. In the past, Tom used a contractor to make his deliveries, but problems arose with damaged merchandise. Now he does the deliveries himself for a small fee; however, Tom's busy schedule makes it difficult to arrange deliveries.

Marketing

Promotion. CeeBee's mottos are "we tote the note" and "why rent when you can buy for less" these mottos emphasize CeeBee's in house financing policy. Tom advertises no credit check and easy payments in his promotions as well. His advertisements appear in the Huntsville Item, the local newspaper, in the TDCJ bucks, a coupon book; in the Spotlight, a free entertainment magazine for county residents and visitors; in TV Guide and on local radio. CeeBee's mainly uses coupons in its advertisements. Tom feels that word of mouth is his greatest advertisement. Tom is an active member of the community which is a good source for him to reach the potential customers.

Price. CeeBee's offers unique services by offering no credit check, in-house financing, low down payments and payment schedules with a maximum of six months. This policy attracts customers who cannot afford to shop at the other local furniture stores, but some of these customers do not make their payments and this has caused CeeBee's to have a high accounts receivable account.

CeeBee's average prices are very comparable to competitor William's Furniture and lower than Adam's Furniture. CeeBee's coupons give the customer discounts off their total purchase. In addition, if the customer chooses to finance their purchase they receive an additional ten percent discount every month that their payments are made on time.

Place. CeeBee's provides the customer with readily available products. The customer can purchase and take home their merchandise in the same day. If the customers orders from the catalog the product is available to them within 5 to 10 days.

Product. CeeBee's primarily sells furniture and appliances and some accessories like centerpieces and lamps. Tom would like to add wide screen television, electronics and entertainment centers because many customers have expressed interest in purchasing them. New products will give CeeBee's a competitive advantage, adding variety to the showroom selection and possibly attracting new customers.

These higher priced products, however, could create risk and problems for CeeBee's. Their purchase would require CeeBee's to borrow to obtain this merchandise, and higher prices may alter CeeBee's image as a discount retailer. In addition, higher prices mean higher customer bills and this could increase the amount of delinquent accounts.

Finance

Furniture and appliance retail sales in Huntsville have followed an increasing trend. The whole industry has increased 37.33% since 1991. In 1996, Huntsville's retail sales for furniture were $7.5 million dollars as compared to $6.2 million in 1995. CeeBee's sales growth over the last two years has been 43.7% per year. Tom attributes this growth to his increased expenditures on advertising by 76% from 1995 to 1996 (see Exhibit 7-2).

CeeBee's accounts receivables make up, on average, 40% of total sales. In 1995, accounts receivable approximated $56,000. Most of CeeBee's customers choose the six month payment option. Several incentives are offered to encourage timely monthly payments. For example, Tom provides ten percent discounts for on time payments. He also allows the customer to call if payment cannot be made on time. He even has a toll free number for out of town customers to call if their payments will be late. Therefore, these customers can avoid late charges. Tom also has penalties for customers who pay late. For example there is a twenty dollar late fee. Tom also has his new customers list references on the credit application. If the new customer does not make their payments, the references listed on his or her application will lose the ability to have credit at CeeBee's.

Tom often has difficulty collecting some accounts. He treats each delinquent case on an individual basis giving the customer every opportunity to pay their balance. After thirty days, Tom sends a certified letter to the customer requesting payment in full or repossession of the furniture. If the request is ignored, Tom refers the account to a collections agent. If the account is still not paid it is turned over to the Sheriff's Department or District Attorney's office for collection. At this time, Tom posts the name on the past due account on a bulletin board in the office that faces the showroom. This also serves as a deterrent to have an overdue account.

Although CeeBee's has incurred losses of $21,032 and $10,704 respectively for 1995 and 1996, Tom feels that the future looks good for CeeBee's. He remarks, "it's not unusual for new stores to lose money for the first couple of years until they get on their feet."

Future Options

Tom is very optimistic about CeeBee's future. He believes that his unique service of no credit check, in house financing will continue to draw new customers. In addition, Tom believes that Huntsville has a solid economy.

Tom has considered opening a new store in a nearby town or in another "prison" city like Huntsville. He feels that CeeBee's major target market is TDCJ guards, many of whom do not have credit or have bad credit and cannot purchase furniture elsewhere. CeeBee's has also considered expanding into several lines of appliances including wide screen televisions.

Exhibit 7-2 CeeBee's Furniture Outlet

Income Statements

	1995	1996
Sales	$140,324	$201,657
Cost of Goods Sold	$93,510	$120,842
Gross Profit	$46,815	$80,815
Operating Expenses		
Salaries and wages	$13,809	$24,506
Automotive expense	$12,518	$13,586
Advertising	$4,955	$8,739
Bank Charges	$285	$173
Interest Expense	$600	
Dues and Subscriptions	$200	$110
Meals and Entertainment	$406	$256
Insurance	$919	$3,852
Legal and Accounting	$250	$230
Office Expense	$24,477	$2,469
Supplies	$2,360	$2,236
Travel	$158	$284
Utilities	$4,799	$27,536
Depreciation	$2,112	
Total deductions	$67,847	$91,519
Ordinary income	($21,032)	(10,704)

Exhibit 7-3 CeeBee's Furniture Outlet

Balance Sheet as of 12-31-95

Cash in Bank	$1,639.72		
Cash on Hand	$923.74		
Cash in Bank Pl.	$98.74		
Judgments Due	$604.00		
Accounts Receivable Sales Tax	$4,116.09		
Inventory	$9,155.21		
Deposits Rent Building 75N	$760.00		
Trailer $1,511.52			
Office Equipment	$600.00		
Total Assets		$19,409.02	

Liabilities:

Sales Tax Payable	$4,116.09	
Visa Payable	$1,181.05	
Total Liabilities		$5,297.14

Partners Capital:

Tom	Investments	$12,763.68	
	Investments Mileage	$2,880.00	
	Investments Guarantee Pymts	$4,500.00	
	Adjust Capital	($442.20)	
	Draws	($1,309.14)	
	50% Net Income	($10,516.12)	
	Net		$7,876.22
Carl	Investments	$6,904.03	
	Investments Pl	$5,347.64	
	Investments Pl	$2,287.87	
	Investments Mileage	$3,215.00	
	Adjust Capital	($442.21)	
	Draws	($560.54)	
	50% Net Income	($10,516.12)	
	Net		$6,235.67

Total Partners Equity		$14,111.88
Total Liability & Equity		$19,409.02